MIX AND MATCH
GARDENING

MIX AND MATCH
GARDENING

Lindsay Thomas

A QUARTO BOOK

First edition for the United States and Canada published in 1998
by Barron's Educational Series, Inc.

All inquiries should be addressed to:
Barron's Educational Series, Inc.
250 Wireless Boulevard
Hauppauge, NY 11788-3917
http://www.barronseduc.com

This book was designed and produced by
Quarto Publishing plc
The Old Brewery
6 Blundell Street
London N7 9BH

Senior editor Anna Watson
Text editor Jane Cavolina
Senior art editor Francis Cawley
Designer Karin Skånberg
Illustrators Elizabeth Dowle, Anne Savage and Ian Sidaway
Photographers Paul Forrester, Peter Stiles
Picture researcher Gill Metcalfe
Editorial manager Sally MacEachern
Art director Moira Clinch

Library of Congress No.: 98-6395
International Standard Book No.: 0-7641-5118-5

Library of Congress Cataloging-in-Publication Data

Thomas, Lindsay, 1952-
        Mix and match gardening / Lindsay Thomas. - Ist ed.
                p.   cm.
        Includes index
        ISBN 0-7641-5118-5
1. Landscape gardening. 2. Gardens—Designs and plans.
3. Landscape plants. I. Title.
SB473. T54 1998
712' .6—dc21   98-6395
                                               CIP

Typeset in Great Britain by
Central Southern Typesetters, Eastbourne
Manufactured in Hong Kong by Regent Publishing Services Ltd
Printed in China by Leefung-Asco Printers Ltd

CONTENTS

Planting a Garden

Relaxing in a lovely garden has to be one of life's great pleasures, but few people are lucky enough to take over a perfect garden. Most of us have to design and plant our gardens before we can sit and enjoy them. For very busy or inexperienced gardeners this can be a daunting task.

IT IS TEMPTING to try to fill a garden the way you would furnish a room, but choosing plants for a garden is not simply a matter of going to the nursery and buying a selection of plants that look appealing. Most people try that approach, and it rarely succeeds.

The difference between furnishing your house and furnishing your garden with plants has to do with time. Chairs and tables are finished items; they do not change dramatically as time passes. Plants, on the other hand, are living, growing organisms; therefore, creating a planting plan is a real challenge.

For each plant you buy, you have to know the eventual shape and size and how its characteristics change with the seasons and through the years. You need to know if it will thrive in the situation you have in mind, and then you have to visualize how it will look with other plants. That is quite a lot to consider at once.

This book is designed to take the hard work and disappointment out of designing a planting scheme by grouping plants that enjoy similar growing conditions and by combining them to complement each other. All you have to do is decide what the conditions are like in your bed or border, and then find the plan that appeals to you.

A CONTEMPORARY GARDEN using modern materials and bold plants, such as the tall *Acanthus* in the foreground. An individual style has been created with the unusual black and gold seat, and a planter constructed using sawn logs.

A MUCH MORE traditional style, with formal box hedging. The planting relies more on architectural structure than on individual plants, and the unifying white paintwork contrasts with the greenery to give a sophisticated, yet relaxed, atmosphere.

ANNUALS grow from seed, flower, shed seeds, and die, all in the space of one growing season. They are useful for instant, dramatic effects, and are a cheap and cheerful way to cover the ground.

BIENNIALS produce foliage in the first year, and flower, seed, and die in the next. They are used for seasonal interest in much the same way as annuals.

PERENNIALS live longer and do not die after producing seed. Some only last for a few years, while others, with the right treatment, go on for many years.

HERBACEOUS PERENNIALS die back to their roots during the winter, leaving more or less bare soil. Other perennials are evergreen and keep their leaves all through the year. They all reach maturity quite quickly, and make an impact a season or two after planting.

SHRUBS AND TREES are woody plants with a presence above ground all year, although deciduous ones lose their leaves in winter. Shrubs are generally smaller; they may have many stems or branch from one stem near ground level. Trees are taller, with one main stem. Woody plants are slow to reach their full size, especially evergreen types. They make the essential framework of the planting.

SUB SHRUBS are a halfway house between perennials and shrubs, being woody only at the base. In cooler regions they are used like perennials.

Because they grow much more slowly, and are the longest lived, it is important to place trees and shrubs with lots of thought. Most can be moved after planting if you make a mistake, but almost always suffer a check to their progress. It is better by far to get it right the first time.

Perennials are much easier to move. In fact, some need to be lifted and split regularly in order to flower well.

When putting plants in the ground, start with the slowest growing, larger ones, making sure they are sited correctly according to your

BUYING PLANTS

When buying plants, it is important to know what sort of life span they are likely to have in order for you to plan how the border will look in years to come.

A FINE EXAMPLE of a mixed planting. Structure is provided by the variegated *Eleagnus* and the *Viburnum* in the center. A contrast in leaf form is provided by the grass. Perennials and deciduous shrubs fill the borders, while at ground level, tender bedding plants fill gaps and provide bright color.

plans, and that they will have enough room to grow unimpeded. Then put in the smaller, quicker growing woody plants. Plant the perennials next, and fill the gaps with annuals and biennials.

As the planting matures, you will find that some perennials will need to be moved around or taken out altogether, but with luck the shrubs and trees can be left in peace to grow and flourish.

MICROCLIMATES

If you are renovating the garden and are planning to buy new plants, it is important to get to know the growing conditions first. You will already know what sort of weather to expect, but every garden has its own microclimates.

IN A NEW garden, you should wait a whole year and note which areas of the garden are sunny and which are shady. This will change with the seasons because the winter sun is far lower in the sky and casts more shade.

Some parts of the garden will be wetter than others, perhaps due to the existence of a water course, to rainwater running off buildings, or to differences in soil types. Soil water content can also change with the seasons.

Dry spots in the garden are usually found near established trees or hedges, at the bases of walls or fences, or where structures prevent rain from reaching the ground.

Wind can seriously affect how plants grow. Try to discover where the sheltered spots are and where the wind is strongest or most turbulent. In exposed gardens you will have to consider how to protect plants, or choose only plants that will tolerate windy conditions.

In frost-prone areas there may be spots in the garden that are especially cold. This is because cold air is heavy and flows downhill like water, collecting at low points or "frost pockets." You will save a lot of disappointment

THE WALLS AND eaves of your house can create sheltered spots which are suitable for growing flowers that might be damaged by rain storms.

if you recognize these places, and plant them only with very hardy species.

Look at all the conditions in your garden and see how they interact to create different microclimates. Once you have discovered them all, the next stage is to investigate the soil itself.

THE AREA AROUND a pond will have its own microclimate, with higher moisture levels than the rest of your garden.

SOIL TYPES

The soil type will usually depend on the geology of the region, but every garden has its own variations, depending on the amount of cultivation, how the soil was treated when the house was built, and the original land use.

ONE IMPORTANT FACTOR is soil pH. This is a measure of how acid or alkaline the soil is, on a scale of 1 to 14. Neutral soil has a pH of 7, alkaline soil has a higher pH, and acid soil a lower pH. Simple and inexpensive soil testing kits can be bought at a garden center. Knowing the pH of your soil is vital, because many plants are fussy and will not thrive if the soil pH is not suited to their needs.

Soil structure will also affect how plants grow. Your soil's structure is determined by the size of the mineral particles, and by the amount of organic matter present.

Sandy soils have large grains that can be felt when rubbed between finger and thumb. They are light to work, warm up quickly, but lose water and nutrients quickly, too. Clay soils have very fine particles. They are heavy to work and take longer to warm up in spring. They may hold too much water, but are fertile.

In between these two extremes are loamy soils. They have a balanced mix of particle sizes, making them fertile, well drained, yet water retentive. Organic matter can improve all soil types. It can help sandy soils retain moisture and nutrients, and it can "open" clay

COASTAL LANDSCAPES CAN be exposed to searing, salt- and sand-laden winds, yet some plants can survive. Here, sea buckthorn (*Hippophaë rhamnoïdes*) is thriving above the strand line. Planting success depends on choosing plants to suit the conditions.

IN CONTRAST, THE shelter of tall trees, deep humus-rich soil, and dappled shade provide ideal growing conditions for rhododendrons and woodland perennials.

soils making them easier to work and more hospitable for growing roots.

Inspect your soil closely. A dark, crumbly soil with lots of organic matter will grow the widest range of plants, but if your soil does not match up to the ideal, don't despair. Soils can be improved, and bear in mind that plants grow almost everywhere. It follows that almost every situation has plants that will grow there. On the whole, the problem is not finding enough plants to suit a site, but being able to restrict the choice to a reasonable number.

PLANT CHARACTERISTICS

For many people the first consideration when buying a plant is its flowers—how big they are, how long they last, and what color they are. Flowers are wonderful, but plants have far more to offer. The overall shape of a plant can play a far more important role in the look of a garden than its flowers, which may only last a few days.

THERE IS NOT a flower in sight in this border, but the leaf colors and shapes create a really effective picture. The elegant purple *Acer palmatum* hangs over striped, grass-like *Liriope* leaves, variegated Pachysandra and the marbled, arrow head leaves of an *Arum italicum*

PLANTS COME IN a multitude of shapes and forms. They may be prostrate, rounded, upright, weeping, arching, open, or dense, and all these forms should be considered in the design of a successful border.

Leaves contribute to the look of a plant grouping for much longer than the flowers, so choosing plants for their leaf qualities makes a lot of sense. They come in many subtly different shades of green, as well as other, more striking colors. They may have attractive variegation, or veins in contrasting colors. Flower color can be greatly enhanced by the complementary or contrasting foliage of nearby plants. The combinations are endless, and some of the most successful plantings are based on leaf contrasts alone.

Variegation is a very useful way of introducing color when no flowers are in bloom. White and yellow variegated leaves can enliven many plantings, especially in shade, or when out-of-bloom plants might have otherwise dull leaves.

Leaf color often changes during the year, too, bringing added seasons of interest. Some plants have differently colored young leaves, and of course there are many that take on wonderful colors in the fall. Evergreens can have changing foliage color as well. New growth often has a different color, and many take on tints with changing weather conditions.

Leaf size is an important characteristic, too. Big leaves make dramatic, architectural statements in a planting, while tiny or finely divided leaves can create an airy, delicate look.

Leaf shape can be used to good effect in a plant grouping. The large, round leaves of *Bergenia*, for instance, make a solid, anchoring statement at the front of a border, while the stiff, upright spikes of *Phormium* have quite a different effect. When placing plants in a border, the way you arrange different leaf sizes may lift an ordinary border to make it something special.

It is often worth considering leaf texture. Shiny leaves reflect light and bring welcome sparkle to many shady situations. Rough or nonreflective leaf surfaces can offer a suitable contrast to flowers and foliage by acting as a backdrop. Many famous herbaceous borders have yew hedges in the background. Leaf texture or detail may be of interest in its own right. The venation, hairiness, or aroma when crushed all add to the interest a plant has to offer, and should not be overlooked when choosing plants.

Twigs and stems often provide interest, especially in deciduous plants. Colored stems are useful when creating winter interest plantings. The dogwoods (*Cornus*) are often used, but there are many others. *Acer palmatum* 'Sango-kaku' is a striking example, and the white stems of silver birch or *Rubus cockburnianus* are great for dramatic effect in dull winter landscapes. The form of twigs and stems is also a useful design tool. The twisted twigs of *Corylus avellana* 'Contorta' are wonderful against a winter sky. Upright, tabular, or drooping twigs can create other interesting effects.

Leaf and flower buds can also be interesting. The sticky buds of horse chestnut, or the black buds of ash are well known, but many garden plants have buds that are special features. For example, *Viburnum tinus* and many *Skimmia* species have attractive overwintering buds.

Some flowers are fleeting but leave fruits or seedheads. Plants that flower in spring and then have colorful fruit in fall are useful, making them two-season plants. *Pyracantha* and *Cotoneaster* are two, but there are many others. Seedheads may not be as colorful as fruits, but they often have great textural

qualities. The fluffy seedheads of *Pulsatilla vulgaris*, or the plumes of *Miscanthus* provide interest for a long time. Fruits and seeds also attract birds and insects, bringing movement and sound to your garden.

Getting to know what plants have to offer besides flowers, and then combining them to create living, interacting compositions is the key to all successful planting designs.

FLOWERS ARE NOT the only attractive attribute of garden plants. Leaf color, shape and texture may all be used to create appealing plant associations. Look out for plants that have a range of characteristics that will be useful for more than one season, such as stem color, bark, and fruits.

USING A GARDEN PLAN

Once you have chosen the plants you wish to buy, the next stage is to consider how many to buy of each. It helps if you have measured the patch of land that is to be planted, either by pacing it out or, more accurately, with a tape measure.

FIRST, CONSIDER THE largest and slowest growing plants. They will be making the most impact, and should have their positions determined carefully. Look at the Plant Directory to find the height and spread guide, then pace or measure a circle to correspond to their eventual size. Ideally this should be marked out on the soil surface with a stick in the center. When the main plants have their positions marked in this way, the spaces and gaps for the smaller plants become apparent. The circles you mark out may overlap, especially where trees are involved, because their height will allow for smaller plants underneath.

Placing the perennials need not be as precise, as they are usually easier to move.

WHEN CHOOSING PLANTS to fill a border it is useful to have a picture in your mind. Sketches of the mature border may help if you are not experienced. Plants can be drawn in roughly after consulting gardening books to choose species and determine shape, eventual size, and so on.

Instead, time and expense are the main considerations. The more plants of each type you put in, the quicker the results, but the greater the cost. Deciding how many of each type of plant is, therefore, a compromise between budget and patience. Cramming plants in covers the ground quickly, but there is a danger that some plants will be overwhelmed. Others may not have the room to develop their best shape. Overcrowded borders may need a lot of maintenance to keep them looking their best. Experienced gardeners allocate generous spaces for the most important plants in a scheme, and use temporary, disposable ones to disguise the bare soil until the "specials" grow to fill their spaces.

The safest way to plan a new planting is to draw a scale plan, and mark out circles to represent the plants. This can be translated into a planting list to take to a nursery or garden center. On the other hand, many people find that the unplanned digging of plants into any available spaces, with varying degrees of success, is a far more satisfying experience. There are no hard and fast rules, and most gardeners develop their own methods with experience.

❶ Fremontodendron 'California Glory'
This produces showy yellow flowers over a long period in summer. It has scaly leaves and stems that may irritate the skin.

❷ Acacia pravissima
The *Acacia* is an arching large shrub or small tree. It has stems well clothed with evergreen, three-sided leaves, and fragrant fluffy yellow flowers in late winter and early spring.

❸ Rhamnus alaternus 'Argenteovariegatus'
Rhamnus is also an evergreen with small variegated leaves and yellow-green flowers in early summer. Red berries that turn black are often borne later in the year. It can be clipped to size.

❹ Ribes laurifolium
Ribes laurifolium is an evergreen with a low, spreading shape, and yellow-green flowers hanging in clusters in late winter.

❺ Ceanothus 'Marie Simon'
The *Ceanothus* has pink flowers in late summer. It is deciduous and may be cut hard back in spring.

❻ Hibiscus syriacus 'Mauve Queen'
This *Hibiscus* has large, pale violet flowers with a darker center, carried in late summer and early fall. The shrub is upright and spreading.

HOW TO USE THIS BOOK

Each spread shows a suggestion for a garden plan at the top of the pages, and the directory of 250 garden plants which are used in the book flows alphabetically along the bottoms of the pages.

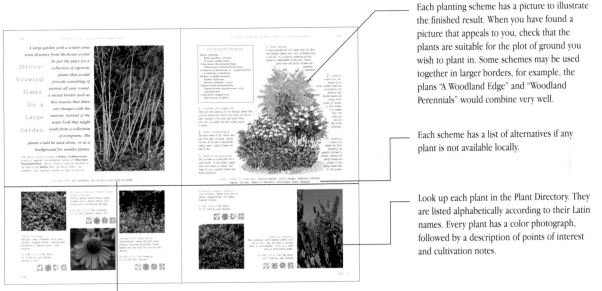

Each planting scheme has a picture to illustrate the finished result. When you have found a picture that appeals to you, check that the plants are suitable for the plot of ground you wish to plant in. Some schemes may be used together in larger borders, for example, the plans "A Woodland Edge" and "Woodland Perennials" would combine very well.

Each scheme has a list of alternatives if any plant is not available locally.

Look up each plant in the Plant Directory. They are listed alphabetically according to their Latin names. Every plant has a color photograph, followed by a description of points of interest and cultivation notes.

Each plan has a note of the soil type and aspect that will give the best results.

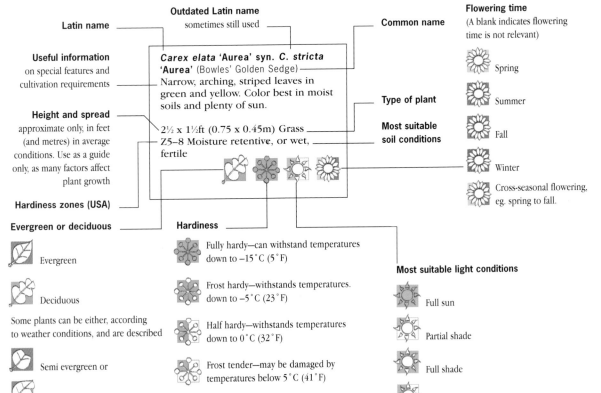

Latin name

Outdated Latin name
sometimes still used

Common name

Flowering time
(A blank indicates flowering time is not relevant)

Useful information
on special features and cultivation requirements

Carex elata 'Aurea' syn. C. stricta 'Aurea' (Bowles' Golden Sedge)
Narrow, arching, striped leaves in green and yellow. Color best in moist soils and plenty of sun.

Spring

Summer

Type of plant

Most suitable soil conditions

Height and spread
approximate only, in feet (and metres) in average conditions. Use as a guide only, as many factors affect plant growth

2½ x 1½ft (0.75 x 0.45m) Grass
Z5–8 Moisture retentive, or wet, fertile

Fall

Winter

Cross-seasonal flowering, eg. spring to fall.

Hardiness zones (USA)

Evergreen or deciduous

Hardiness

Evergreen

Fully hardy—can withstand temperatures down to –15˚C (5˚F)

Deciduous

Frost hardy—withstands temperatures. down to –5˚C (23˚F)

Most suitable light conditions

Some plants can be either, according to weather conditions, and are described

Half hardy—withstands temperatures down to 0˚C (32˚F)

Full sun

Partial shade

Semi evergreen or

Frost tender—may be damaged by temperatures below 5˚C (41˚F)

Full shade

Evergreen/deciduous.

Sun or partial shade

An All-Year Plan

Creating an all-year border in a small space means choosing plants that are either good to look at in all seasons, or that make an important contribution for part of the year and then provide a background for other times. This is quite difficult to get right because the look depends on a balance of shapes as well as seasons of interest.

This collection is an illustration of how to plant up a peninsular bed to achieve the effect. It has a good outline all year round and yet changes throughout the year.

THE BARE, TWISTED TWIGS of *Corylus avellana* 'Contorta' provide interest in the bleakest months, and the pretty catkins dangle and sway in the spring breezes. The leaves that follow are relatively graceless, but with complementary summer interest plants their presence is minimized.

SUITABLE SITUATION: any reasonable soil in an open, sunny position

Abelia × grandiflora
Brittle stems so avoid windy sites. Persistent calyces remain attractive after flowering.

10 x 12ft (3 x 3.7m) Shrub
Z5–9 Fertile, well drained, not very alkaline

Abutilon × suntense
Fast, upright. Gray-green leaves and showy flowers.

12 x 8ft (3.7 x 2.4m) Shrub
Z8–10 Fertile, well drained

Acacia pravissima (Oven's Wattle)
Arching habit, profuse fragrant flowers. Train against a sunny wall for extra warmth.

15 x 15ft (4.6 x 4.6m) Shrub/tree
Z8–10 Fertile, well drained, neutral to acid

❶ *Corylus avellana* 'Contorta'
❷ *Miscanthus sinensis* 'Rotsilber'

This *Corylus* is nicknamed "Harry Lauder's Walking Stick" because of the twisted stems visible in winter. They look especially attractive against the sky in low winter sun and again in spring when hung with yellow catkins. Flower arrangers love it. In summer it has contorted leaves which can look heavy, but are offset here by the airy foliage and flower heads of the *Miscanthus*.

❸ *Erica carnea* 'Myretoun Ruby'
Echoing the shape of the *Buxus* are the hummocks of winter heathers, valuable for winter flowers and evergreen foliage in a wide choice of colors. *Erica carnea* will tolerate some soil alkalinity.

❹ *Buxus sempervirens* 'Elegantissima'
Anchoring the scheme is the solid mass of the *Buxus* which looks good all year with its neat, white-margined leaves. It can be pruned to any shape.

❺ *Lilium* 'Enchantment'
In summer the *Lilium* 'Enchantment', not shown in this winter-time picture, will add a splash of color behind the *Bergenia*.

❻ *Bergenia* 'Morgenröte'
An evergreen edge to finish the look is provided by *Bergenia* with its large, tough leaves that may change color in cold weather. It has reddish flowers in early spring.

EXTRA PLANTS TO CONSIDER: *Mahonia* cultivars, *Euonymus*, *Hedera helix* 'Erecta', *Liriope*, *Hebe speciosa*

SPRING BULBS IN A SMALL GARDEN

The dying leaves of spring bulbs take up space in a small garden and look unattractive after the flowers are over. The answer is to plant smaller varieties underneath deciduous shrubs and behind late-emerging perennials. In this plan, bulbs have been planted under a rose. Give the dying foliage of the daffodils and Erythronium *a liquid feed and benefit the rose at the same time.*

A good perennial to grow in front is Geranium wallichianum *'Buxton's Variety'; further back you could grow Japanese anemones for flowers in late summer.*

A GROUP OF DAFFODILS provides early color and interest during the spring months. The bulbs in this plan will cheer up the stems beneath any shrub which remains uninteresting until late spring. Here, the shrub is *Amelanchier,* which is very useful in a small garden. It has pretty spring blossoms followed by colorful leaves and interesting fruit in fall.

SUITABLE SITE: any fertile soil in sun

❶ *Rosa xanthina* 'Canary Bird'

'Canary Bird' is an early rose with single yellow blooms and an elegant, arching habit. The foliage is dainty and ferny, keeping the shrub looking good even after flowering.

Before the foliage on the rose is fully out, the bulbs will be giving their display.

❷ *Erythronium revolutum* Johnsonii Group

The *Erythronium* has low hummocks of leaves with brown mottling. The flowers are large and pink and dangle on wiry stems.

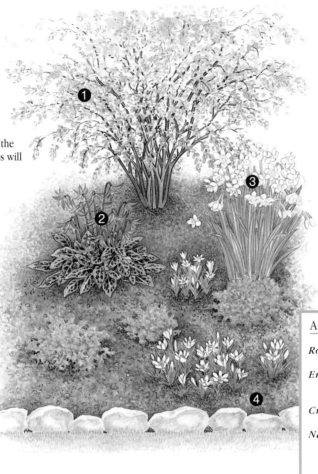

❸ *Narcissus* 'Cheerfulness'

Each stem of the daffodil bears several sweetly scented, double flowers in pale yellow. Deadhead, and feed the foliage and stems to build up the bulbs for next year.

❹ *Crocus vernus* 'Joan of Arc'

The grassy foliage of the crocus bears white flowers with purple bases. If the soil is moist they may benefit from added grit to help with drainage. They are happy on poorer soil, so grow them at the front and don't mulch them with the others.

ALTERNATIVE VARIETIES

Rosa xanthina 'Canary Bird'
　Any tall deciduous shrub
Erythronium revolutum
　Johnsonii Group
　Erythronium revolutum
Crocus vernus 'Joan of Arc'
　Any spring crocus
Narcissus 'Cheerfulness'
　Narcissus 'Yellow
　Cheerfulness'
　(or any shorter daffodil)

EXTRA PLANTS TO CONSIDER: *Amelanchier, Cyclamen coum, Scilla, Iris reticulata, Hyacinthus, Arum italicum* 'Pictum'

A GROUP OF SPRING SHRUBS

This grouping will give a succession of color from late winter to early summer. They will grow on any fertile, humus-rich soil in full sun, but the Chaenomeles *and* Daphne *may become chlorotic on very thin soil over chalk. The symptoms are yellowing of the leaves, especially new ones, and a hungry look to the plants. If this happens, feed and water well then mulch and apply a chemical treatment containing chelated iron. Ask for help at the nursery in choosing one.*

A CEANOTHUS THYRSIFLORUS VAR. REPENS in full bloom beneath a **Viburnum tomentosum** 'Lanarth', and next to a variegated holly. The arrangement of shrubs is graded in height from the level of the lawn up to the trees in the background, enclosing the garden with a wall of interesting flowers and leaves.

SUITABLE SITE: any reasonable soil in full sun

❶ *Syringa* × *josiflexa* 'Bellicent'
This lilac is a large, open shrub with loose panicles of fragrant flowers. It has a more elegant shape than many other lilacs, and the leaves are more attractive.

❷ *Dipelta floribunda*
Dipelta is a deciduous shrub with an upright form and fragrant flowers a little like those of a rhododendron. When mature it has attractive peeling bark, giving extra interest in the winter.

❸ *Chaenomeles* × *superba* 'Knapp Hill Scarlet'
This form of flowering quince is a low-spreading bush bearing scarlet flowers with a boss of golden stamens in spring. Yellowish fruits are often produced later in the year.

❹ *Daphne odora* 'Aureomarginata'
In early spring the *Daphne* bears highly fragrant pink and white flowers. It is low growing and evergreen, making it a good plant to grow in front of the deciduous shrubs.

❺ *Ceanothus thyrsiflorus* var. *repens*
The blue of the spring-flowering *Ceanothus* makes a good contrast to the more usual pinks and yellows of other spring-flowering shrubs. As an evergreen in temperate zones it is also useful at the front of a border.

EXTRA PLANTS TO CONSIDER: *Ribes alpinum* 'Aureum,' *Prunus tenella,* *Spiraea japonica* 'Goldflame,' *Genista lydia*, *Syrina microphylla* 'Superba'

Spring Shrubs with Climbers

The trouble with some flowering shrubs is that they are not particularly attractive for the rest of the year. Deciduous, and with unexciting foliage, they may not justify the space they take up. In small gardens on alkaline soils this may limit the choice for spring color. The solution is to clothe them in clematis

to flower later in the year. Two seasons of color can therefore be had in one space. Clematis is the obvious choice of climber because scrambling through shrubs toward the sun is its natural habit. They enjoy having their roots in shade, but then may be short of nutrients and water. Feed well, water and mulch regularly.

SOME RATHER DULL BRANCHES of a spring flowering cherry are adorned with a *Clematis viticella* 'Abundance', bringing another flush of color in summer. *Viticella* clematis are useful in exposed situations, and where clematis wilt is a problem. They are ideal for growing into trees and shrubs.

SUITABLE SITE: any reasonably fertile soil, acid or alkaline, in sun or partial shade

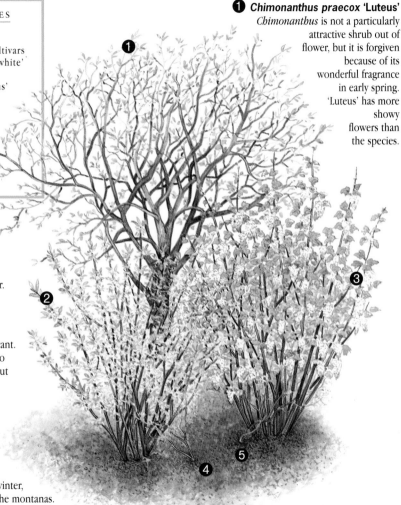

❶ *Chimonanthus praecox* 'Luteus'
Chimonanthus is not a particularly attractive shrub out of flower, but it is forgiven because of its wonderful fragrance in early spring. 'Luteus' has more showy flowers than the species.

❷ *Forsythia* 'Beatrix Farrand'
The sight of *Forsythia* in bloom is always welcome, with its bright yellow blossom on bare twigs. It is good for cutting, and this one has some fall color.

**❸ *Ribes sanguineum*
'Tydeman's White'**
Ribes is the ever-popular flowering currant. A white cultivar has been chosen here to look better with the fading *Forsythia*, but a pink cultivar would be fine.

❹ *Clematis* 'Etoile Violette'
❺ *Clematis* 'Alba Luxurians'
The clematis are both viticella types, ideal for growing into shrubs, but because they are best cut back to buds just above ground at the end of every winter, they never overwhelm their hosts like the montanas.

EXTRA PLANTS TO CONSIDER: *Philadelphus, Deutzia, Syringa, Clematis rehderiana, Clematis tangutica*

EASY SUMMER SHRUBS

If you would like lots of summer flowers but would rather not spend a lot of time on maintenance, then this combination of shrubs blooms all summer long with very little attention. There is a good evergreen background, and the deciduous shrubs, Lavatera and Buddleia, provide contrasts in shape as well as flower. They only require a good cutting back in early spring.

The Escallonia, Choisya and Cistus do not need regular pruning, and the lavender need only be clipped lightly as soon as flowering is over.

LAVATERA ARBOREA AND BUDDLEIA 'Black Knight' make a rich backdrop for a low-growing mixed planting. *Hypericum* is also an easy shrub. There are two varieties in this border, one in full bloom beneath the *Lavatera*, and the other in the foreground showing its dark red fruits.

SUITABLE SITE: any reasonable soil in sun, sheltered from cold winds

ALTERNATIVE VARIETIES

Escallonia 'Donard Beauty'
    Any hardy *Escallonia*
Lavatera thuringiaca 'Barnsley'
    Lavatera olbia 'Rosea'
Buddleia davidii 'Dartmoor'
    Buddleia davidii cultivars
Lavandula angustifolia 'Munstead'
    Lavandula angustifolia 'Hidcote'
Choisya ternata 'Sundance'
    Spiraea japonica 'Goldflame
Cistus 'Grayswood Pink'
    Cistus × purpureus

② *Lavatera thuringiaca* 'Barnsley'
③ *Buddleia davidii* 'Dartmoor'
Lavatera is an accommodating shrub that will flower prolifically all summer, even when neglected, and has the look of an arching hollyhock. It associates well with *Buddleia davidii* and tolerates the same treatment. Prune them both to buds a few inches above ground level in spring to keep them looking graceful.

① *Escallonia* 'Donard Beauty'
Escallonia can tolerate the warmer, salt-laden winds of mild coastal areas and is useful as protection in those areas. In colder areas some of the more tender varieties will resent bitter winds, so choose carefully. They are not happy on highly alkaline soil.

④ *Lavandula angustifolia* 'Munstead'
Lavenders look good all year if trimmed correctly, making neat gray, aromatic cushions, but their moment of glory comes when the blue-purple flowers open to give off that wonderfully evocative perfume.

⑤ *Choisya ternata* 'Sundance'
The *Choisya ternata* 'Sundance' is a bright yellow evergreen that will look well against the darker green of the *Escallonia*. It has aromatic leaves and fragrant, white flowers in summer, and sometimes sporadically into the fall.

⑥ *Cistus* 'Grayswood Pink'
Cistus 'Grayswood Pink' has salmon pink flowers above gray-green evergreen foliage that contrasts well with the other evergreens.

EXTRA PLANTS TO CONSIDER: *Olearia, Deutzia, Spiraea*

A Mixed Border for the Summer

This border has contrasting flower shapes and colors, and would look and smell lovely from late spring right through to the fall. But in the winter it has little interest. Beds of this sort are best placed where they are not closely viewed from the house in the coldest months. Or, if they can't be hidden away, winter interest plants should be planted to draw the eye away.

CYTISUS BATTANDIERI GROWING harmoniously on a wall with *Phlomis fruticosa* at its feet. The yellow rose on the other wall, and the creamy *Sisyrinchium striatum* in the foreground continue the color theme in this sunny seating area. The *Sisyrinchium* is a useful upright perennial that seeds itself around when growing happily.

SUITABLE SITE: well-drained soil of moderate fertility, in a sunny spot

❶ Cytisus battandieri

This is an unusual *Cytisus* in that it has broad, silvery-green leaves that are semi-evergreen. It is a wide-spreading shrub with yellow upright flowers that smell of pineapple.

❷ Buddleia globosa

Buddleia globosa gets its name from the spherical flowers borne in early summer. They are orange and sweet smelling, and the shrub itself is large and vigorous, best pruned hard after flowering.

ALTERNATIVE VARIETIES

Cytisus battandieri
   Cytisus battandieri 'Yellow Tail'
   Cytisus 'Lena'
Buddleia globosa
   Buddleia × *weyeriana*
Ceanothus thyrsiflorus var. *repens*
   Ceanothus 'Yankee Point'
Phlomis fruticosa
   Phlomis russeliana
Alstroemeria aurea
   Alstroemeria aurea cultivars

---

❺ Alstroemeria aurea

The perennial *Alstroemeria* has stems of narrow leaves topped by lily-like flowers in orange. It can run, but should not worry the *Phlomis* or the *Buddleia*.

❸ Ceanothus thyrsiflorus var. repens

This *Ceanothus* is evergreen and mound forming, with powder-blue, thimble-shaped flowers in spring and early summer. It is a good front-of-border shrub.

❹ Phlomis fruticosa

A gray contrast in the planting is provided by the *Phlomis*. It has woolly leaves that are almost white underneath. Whorls of yellow flowers appear over the summer and persist as attractive seedheads.

EXTRA PLANTS TO CONSIDER: *Helianthemum, Heliopsis, Caryopteris, Ceratostigma*

LATE SUMMER PERENNIALS

As the summer grows hotter and the sun gets higher in the sky, spring foliage loses its freshness, and pale colors look bleached. The abundance of early summer grows tired looking. Strong colors and bold shapes are needed. These late summer flowers in red and yellow are bright enough to lift a herbaceous border with late summer color. Not only do they have contrasting leaf and flower forms, but they also blend with the impending colors of the fall.

STRONG COLORS IN BOLD clumps stand up to harsh, high summer sunlight, and the greens of the surrounding foliage make difficult juxtapositions of reds and oranges work. In this picture two sides of a fence are linked visually by bright flowers. Contrasting leaf types provide further interest.

SUITABLE SITE: fertile, moisture-retaining soil in full sun

ALTERNATIVE VARIETIES

Solidago 'Goldenmosa'
   Solidago 'Golden Wings'
   Solidago 'Queenie' syn. 'Golden Thumb'
Heliopsis helianthoïdes 'Light of Loddon'
   Heliopsis helianthoïdes 'Ballerina'
Helenium 'Waldtraut'
   Helenium 'The Bishop'
   Helenium 'Riverton Beauty'
Kniphofia rooperi
   Kniphofia caulescens
Crocosmia 'Lucifer'
   Crocosmia 'Bressingham Blaze'
X *Solidaster luteus*
   X *Solidaster luteus*
   'Lenmore'

❶ Solidago 'Goldenmosa'
This *Solidago* is compact and bushy and bears bright yellow flowers in conical panicles during late summer and early fall.

❷ Helenium 'Waldtraut'
Helenium 'Waldraut' is upright and sturdy with flowers in golden yellow and brown.

❸ Heliopsis helianthoïdes 'Light of Loddon'
Heliopsis has semi-double flowers in conical flower heads borne above dark green leaves. It looks good at the back of a border.

❹ Crocosmia 'Lucifer'
'Lucifer' is a bright red, tall *Crocosmia* blooming from midsummer.

❺ X Solidaster luteus
X *Solidaster luteus* has flower heads of pale yellow daisy-like flowers.

❻ Kniphofia rooperi
Kniphofia rooperi is almost evergreen with yellow-orange to red flowers.

EXTRA PLANTS TO CONSIDER: asters, dahlias, chrysanthemums

THE APTLY NAMED *PHYGELIUS aequalis* 'Yellow Trumpet' seems to glow in the sunlight. Its soft, creamy yellow is easy to place with other colors in a mixed border. If not grown next to a warm wall, cut it to ground level in winter like other perennials.

LATE SUMMER

IN A

SHELTERED SPOT

If you have a warm, sheltered spot where frost and sharp winds are unlikely, then growing something "different" is possible. This collection of late-flowering plants will thrive against a sheltered, sunny wall giving color and perfume well into the fall. Prepare the soil well, ensuring that it has plenty of humus to prevent it drying out. Abelia *and* Hibiscus *will not thrive on extreme alkalinity. Apply a dry mulch if cold weather is predicted.*

SUITABLE SITE: sunny and sheltered, on neutral to acid soil

❶ Abelia × grandiflora

Abelia × grandiflora is evergreen in mild situations. The small, shiny leaves set off the pinky white flowers, and the long-lasting pink calyces are colorful long after flowering has finished.

❷ Crinum × powellii

Lax, strap-like leaves and stout stems of *Crinum* bear fragrant flowers reminiscent of pink lilies. They must be planted with the necks of the bulbs protruding slightly above the soil.

❸ Hibiscus syriacus 'Mauve Queen'

Upright and arching, the *Hibiscus* looks good against a wall with the pale yellow *Phygelius* beneath. The flowers are very showy with protruding stigma and stamens in wide-flaring petals.

❹ Phygelius aequalis 'Yellow Trumpet'

Also prone to spreading if suited, the *Phygelius* has pale green leaves and elegant panicles of pale yellow flowers.

❺ Clerodendrum bungei

Clerodendrum bungei spreads by suckers and will need to be checked if it threatens nearby plants. Heart-shaped leaves are a good foil for the magenta domes of very fragrant flowers.

EXTRA PLANTS TO CONSIDER: *Clematis rehderiana*, *Lonicera* periclymenum 'Serotina', *Galtonia*, *Ceanothus* 'Marie Simon', *Zauschneria*, *Eccremocarpus scaber*

WINTER HIGHLIGHTS

This grouping has an all-year presence with highlights to brighten the gloom of winter. It would suit any humus-rich soil in sun or partial shade. The Gaultheria really does need to be in acid soil, but the scheme will still work if you substitute a group of skimmias for the Gaultheria, to suit a neutral to alkaline soil. Male and female skimmias are both needed for berries to be produced.

A SIMPLE, YET ELEGANT winter planting. Two varieties of *Hamamelis* stand out against the evergreens behind, and bring welcome winter color to a parterre of dwarf box hedging. In summer, when the *Hamamelis* is not in flower, the beds would be filled with various types of bedding plants.

SUITABLE SITE: humus-rich soil in sun or partial shade

❶ *Hamamelis* × *intermedia* 'Pallida'
The *Hamamelis* is a large shrub with fall color and fragrant winter flowers, even in the bitterest weather. In sun it will provide shade for the shade lovers beneath.

❸ *Gaultheria mucronata* 'Cherry Ripe'
Low evergreen cover is provided by *Gaultheria mucronata*. White summer flowers are followed by long-lasting, cerise pink berries. Plant a few as this variety is not as spreading as *Gaultheria shallon* or *Gaultheria procumbens*, and males and females are needed to ensure berrying.

❷ *Mahonia* × *media* 'Charity'
Mahonia × *media* is a large, upright shrub with evergreen leaves in whorls providing architectural form all year. It has eye-catching yellow, fragrant flowers in winter.

ALTERNATIVE VARIETIES

Hamamelis × *intermedia*
    'Pallida'
    Any *Hamamelis* cultivar
Mahonia × *media* 'Charity'
    Mahonia × *media* 'Buckland'
Cornus alba 'Sibirica'
    Cornus alba cultivars
Galanthus nivalis 'Pusey Green Tip'
    Galanthus nivalis
Gaultheria mucronata 'Cherry Ripe'
    Gaultheria mucronata 'Lilacina'
    Gaultheria mucronata 'Bell's Seedling'
On alkaline soil, *Skimmia japonica* cultivars
    Skimmia japonica 'Scarlet Dwarf' or
    'Fructo-albo' (female) with *Skimmia
    japonica* 'Rubella' (male)

❹ *Galanthus nivalis* 'Pusey Green Tip'
In amongst the *Cornus* shoots, and around the taller shrubs, plant snowdrops (*Galanthus nivalis*) to herald the start of spring. 'Pusey Green Tip' really merits close inspection, but any snowdrop will do.

❺ *Cornus alba* 'Sibirica'
A touch of red in winter is provided by the dogwood (*Cornus*). In this arrangement it should be hard pruned each spring to obtain a neat shape and the best coloration. The leaves turn red before falling. In bigger beds try adding dogwoods with stems of different colors.

EXTRA PLANTS TO CONSIDER: *Helleborus, Bergenia, Cyclamen coum, Rubus cockburnianus, Lonicera* × *purpusii, Sarcococcas, Viburnum tinus, Jasminum nudiflorum, Leucojum*

Winter Cherry with Underplanting

The winter-flowering cherry looks wonderful in a lawn on well-drained, even chalky soil. Its pink blossom is a welcome sight in winter, and, as the tree matures, it takes on a venerable shape. Underplant it with low growers to flower at the same time and emphasize its brave display. For the rest of the year it only has its outline and some fall color to recommend it, but then there is plenty of interest in other parts of the garden.

WITHOUT THE BRIGHT PRESENCE of this crocus (*Crocus* × *luteus* 'Golden Yellow') the area around this deciduous shrub would look very bleak, with just bare soil in winter. As the bulbs fade and their foliage begins to look shabby, the leaves of the shrub will be unfolding to take the limelight.

SUITABLE SITE: reasonable soil, neutral to alkaline, in sun or partial shade

ALTERNATIVE VARIETIES

Prunus × subhirtella 'Autumnalis Rosea'
   Magnolia × loebneri 'Leonard Messel'
Helleborus niger
   Helleborus argutifolius
Crocus × luteus 'Golden Yellow' syn.
   Crocus 'Yellow Mammoth'
   Any early-flowering crocus
Anemone blanda
   Anemone nemorosa
Eranthis hyemalis
   Primula vulgaris

❶ *Prunus × subhirtella* 'Autumnalis Rosea'
The winter cherry has bronzy leaves in spring and the flowers may be followed by very dark fruit. The leaves turn yellow before falling.

❸ Eranthis hyemalis
Winter aconites complete the picture with their bright yellow flowers held above neat ruffs of green leaves in late winter. Do not try to pick too many, as it means removing leaves and damaging the plant.

❷ Helleborus niger
Helleborus niger, or Christmas rose, has white, sometimes pink-tinged flowers all winter. They are held above overwintering leaves that are renewed in spring.

❹ Anemone blanda
Anemone blanda will establish large clumps when happy and this one, in particular, will brighten the ground under the cherry with its big white flowers in spring.

❺ *Crocus × luteus* 'Golden Yellow'
This bright yellow crocus is vigorous, and can be naturalized in the grass around the cherry.

EXTRA PLANTS TO CONSIDER: *Hepatica nobilis, Bergenia × schmidtii, Cyclamen coum, Lamium*

AN

ORIENTAL

INFLUENCE

Create a serene, restful area using just foliage plants. This arrangement has echoes of an oriental garden, but would not look out of place in any garden or courtyard. It has shades of green and hints of other colors, but nothing bright or jarring. The interest comes entirely from the juxtaposition of different foliage shapes and textures. Seasonal changes are subtle, but fascinating.

The picture could be individualized by the careful positioning of stones or statuary. Mulching with shingle or gravel would be a nice finishing touch.

A STONE BRIDGE OVER some carefully arranged pebbles and chippings creates the impression of running water in this Japanese-look garden. Foliage contrasts are provided by the yellow *Acer*, blue *Hosta* and palmate leaves of a *Fatsia*. Dwarf conifers and a *Nandina*, or heavenly bamboo, complete the picture.

SUITABLE SITE: moist, humus-rich, acid to neutral soil in partial or full shade. Shelter from cold winds

❶ Acer palmatum 'Sango-kaku'

This small, upright *Acer* has coral-colored new stems in winter and leaves that open orange-yellow in spring, then turn green before coloring up again in the fall.

❷ Fatsia japonica

Fatsia japonica has large, leathery leaves, palmate in shape. It is a rounded shrub, eventually becoming quite big. It is tolerant of pollution, can be wall trained, and makes good screening.

ALTERNATIVE VARIETIES

Acer palmatum 'Sango-kaku'
    Acer palmatum var. *heptalobum*
Fatsia japonica
    Fatsia japonica 'Variegata'
Matteuccia struthiopteris
    Osmunda regalis
Pleioblastus variegatus
    Pleioblastus auricomus syn.
    Arundinaria auricoma
Hosta sieboldiana 'Elegans'
    Hosta sieboldiana
Lysimachia nummularia 'Aurea'
    Lysimachia nummularia

❹ Pleioblastus variegatus

A dwarf bamboo with striped leaves placed in front of the dark *Fatsia* will lighten a potentially heavy look and bring a little movement. It can be tidied by cutting to ground level in spring.

❸ Matteuccia struthiopteris

This deciduous fern has an upright, narrow habit and spreads slowly. The fronds are delicate looking and pretty as they unfurl in spring.

❺ Hosta sieboldiana 'Elegans'

A broad-leaved hosta with blue-gray leaves introduces more color and texture. The flowers are in a quiet lilac-white.

❻ Lysimachia nummularia 'Aurea'

Finally, creeping in among the stones and bases of the other plants, the little round leaves of the golden creeping jenny bring interest at ground level.

EXTRA PLANTS TO CONSIDER: Dwarf conifers, Azaleas, *Camellia*, mosses, *Pratia pedunculata, Soleirolia soleirolii, Milium effusum* 'Aureum', *Nandina*

Consider foliage shape and texture when choosing plants, especially evergreens, whose flowers may be fleeting, leaving only the leaves for the rest of the year.

CAMELLIA WITH FOLIAGE CONTRASTS

The leaves of a camellia are lustrous and light reflective, bringing sparkle to the shady areas that suit them best.

A camellia, with a supporting cast of foliage plants, creates a sophisticated grouping with year-round appeal for a sheltered, shady position.

A CAMELLIA × WILLIAMSII 'DONATION' growing prolifically against an old wall. The flowers are not the only attraction — the leaves are also handsome, making them useful in restricted spaces, and where evergreen interest is needed all year.

SUITABLE SITE: fertile, neutral to acid, humus-rich soil. Sheltered position in shade, or with sun only later in the day

❶ *Jasminum nudiflorum*

Contrasting well with camellia foliage is winter jasmine, with its lax green stems and brave winter flowers. It can be trained up wires and then be allowed to cascade down.

❸ *Bergenia milesii* 'Morgenröte/ Morning Red'

In front of the taller plants, an evergreen edge is provided by *Bergenia* with its leathery, almost round leaves. It has pink flowers in spring and makes good ground cover.

❹ *Liriope muscari*

The grassy, strap-shaped leaves of the *Liriope* look good all year, but especially so with the violet flowers produced in late summer.

❺ *Hosta sieboldiana* 'Frances Williams'

The picture is completed in summer by the variegated leaves of the hosta. It has clumps of puckered leaves in bluey-green and yellow. Placed in front of the camellia the white flowers of the hosta are shown to best effect, and they would both benefit from generous mulching with leaf mold.

❷ *Camellia* × *williamsii* 'Bow Bells'

Camellias are aristocratic shrubs, but this hybrid is small enough to grow near a house wall. Its glossy leaves and fine blooms make it a good all-year shrub. Early morning sun damages the flowers in frosty weather, so don't plant it with an unprotected easterly aspect.

ALTERNATIVE VARIETIES

Camellia × *williamsii* 'Bow Bells'
Camellia × *williamsii* cultivars
Jasminum nudiflorum
Clematis cirrhosa 'Freckles'
Bergenia milesii 'Morgenröte/ Morning Red'
Bergenia cordifolia and cultivars
Liriope muscari
Liriope cultivars
Hosta sieboldiana 'Frances Williams'
Hosta (large-leaved cultivars)

EXTRA PLANTS TO CONSIDER: *Matteuccia struthiopteris, Dicentra* cultivars, *Polygonatum* × *hybridum, Heuchera* cultivars

EXCITING FOLIAGE COLORS

Fertile soil that is reliably moist can support the most attractively lush growth. The plants that have been put together here have contrasting leaf shapes and some dramatic color combinations that would certainly provoke interest and comment. The flowers, too, contribute to make a picture of fiery yellows, oranges and reds.

THE FOLIAGE OF *EUPHORBIA dulcis* 'Chameleon' in fall is colorful enough without flowers, but its small yellow-green flowers are welcome in spring. Exciting effects can be achieved with foliage in hot colors, but plants like this *Euphorbia* are also useful for injecting a bit of color into any border.

SUITABLE SITE: moisture-retentive soil that is fertile and reliably moist in hot weather; full sun

① Berberis thunbergii var. 'Atropurpurea'
The background is provided by the purple-red leaves of the berberis. It has pink-tinged flowers followed by red berries and good, red fall tints. For a toned-down color scheme, use the plain green version.

② Lysimachia ciliata 'Firecracker'
Lysimachia has bronze-purple leaves and simple, yellow flowers in summer.

ALTERNATIVE VARIETIES

Berberis thunbergii var. 'Atropurpurea'
Berberis ottawensis 'Purpurea'
Euphorbia dulcis 'Chameleon'
Euphorbia griffithii 'Fireglow'
Houttuynia cordata 'Chameleon'
Houttuynia cordata
Lysimachia ciliata 'Firecracker'
Lysimachia ciliata 'Purpurea'
Ajuga 'Atropupurea'
Rodgersia pinnata
Rodgersia pinnata 'Superba'
Hemerocallis 'Stafford'
Hemerocallis 'Alan,' 'Berlin Red' 'Ashanti Gold' or 'Amadeus'

③ Rodgersia pinnata
Rodgersia leaves are handsomely dissected into leaflets, and the flowers are fluffy pink fading to persistent, buff seedheads.

④ Euphorbia dulcis 'Chameleon'
For moisture-retentive soil that is fertile and reliably moist in hot weather. Full sun.

⑤ Hemerocallis 'Stafford'
The *Hemerocallis* has strap-shaped leaves that look good, especially when they emerge in spring. The flowers of this variety are a deep mahogany red, but there are many different colors to choose from. If the scheme is too exotic, tone it down by growing less strikingly colored cultivars.

⑥ Houttuynia cordata 'Chameleon'
In suitable soils the *Houttuynia* will run. It has gaudy variegated leaves that smell of citrus when crushed. The flowers are relatively sedate, a demure white.

EXTRA PLANTS TO CONSIDER: *Filipendula, Ligularia, Lysimachia punctata, Lobelia fulgens*

A large border viewed at a distance needs to be bold to hold the attention. Rather than relying on diffuse flower color, sometimes it is better to use strong foliage colors.

This collection of shrubs would suit the back of a large border. It would provide a succession of leaf color changes, beginning at bud break and finishing with leaf fall.

FOLIAGE COLORS IN A LARGE BORDER

The shrubs would look wonderful viewed across a large pond or lake, so that the colors were reflected in the water.

THE SOFT COLOR OF the leaves of this *Acer* reflected in the water creates a tranquil picture. Later, the leaves will change color, bringing drama to the end of the summer. Similar effects are possible in small gardens with even a tiny patch of reflective water.

SUITABLE SITE: acid soil that is humus-rich and moisture-retentive. Partial shade

❶ *Cotinus coggygria* 'Royal Purple'

'Royal Purple' is a variety of *Cotinus* that has rich purple-red leaves. Fluffy red flowers appear in late summer. It may be cut back in spring to promote bigger leaves, but will mean a loss of flowers for that year.

❷ *Robinia pseudoacacia* 'Frisia'

This cultivar is a smaller tree than the plain species *Robinia pseudoacacia,* and has bright greenish yellow leaves that turn clear yellow in the fall.

❸ *Physocarpus opulifolius* 'Luteus'

Physocarpus is an upright shrub with red new stem growth and golden-yellow leaves. Grow it out of strong sunlight to avoid scorching.

❺ *Sorbus reducta*

Sorbus reducta is a creeping mountain ash. Low growing and spreading, it has gray-green leaves that turn bronzy red in fall. White flowers in summer are followed by pink berries.

❹ *Acer palmatum* Dissectum Atropurpureum Group

This is a lower-growing shrub with an arching habit. It has beautifully divided and colored foliage, starting deep purple and turning to shades of orange and red in the fall.

EXTRA PLANTS TO CONSIDER: *Hamamelis, Amelanchier, Fothergilla, Euonymus alatus*

STRONG-GROWING PLANTS FOR A LARGE GARDEN

A large garden with a wilder area some distance from the house would be just the place for a collection of vigorous plants that would provide something of interest all year round. A mixed border such as this ensures that there are changes with the seasons, instead of the static look that might result from a collection of evergreens. The plants could be used alone, or as a background for smaller plants.

THE WHITE WINTER STEMS of *Rubus Cockburnianus* stand out against the evergreen leaves of *Viburnum rhytidophyllum*. White, winter flowering heathers at the feet of the *Rubus* echo the white stems, but remember that heathers prefer an open situation.

SUITABLE SITE: any reasonably fertile soil in sun or partial shade

ALTERNATIVE VARIETIES

Rhus typhina
  Rhus glabra 'Laciniata'
  Prunus subhirtella
Viburnum rhytidophyllum
  Viburnum cinnamomifolium
Sorbaria tomentosa var. *angustifolia*
  Sorbaria sorbifolia
Rubus cockburnianus
  Rubus biflorus
  Betula pendla 'Youngii'
Eupatorium purpureum
  Eupatorium purpureum subsp.
  maculatum
Sinacalia tanguticus
  Macleaya cordata

❶ *Rhus typhina*

A large spreading shrub or small tree, the *Rhus* has handsome leaves that color up dramatically in the fall. It is prone to suckering and thus suited to a large border of this sort. Female plants have red conical flowers and persistent seedheads.

❷ Sorbaria tomentosa var. angustifolia

Stout, upright stems are produced by the *Sorbaria* with divided leaves and creamy white plumes of flowers in late summer. It is invasive when the conditions suit, but fine in this collection.

❸ Viburnum rhytidophyllum

Viburnum rhytidophyllum has drooping leaves that could be dispiriting close to the house, but are an ideal contrast to the other leaf forms. White buds last all winter and open creamy yellow in spring.

❹ Rubus cockburnianus

The white stems of the *Rubus* are a real focal point in winter. During the rest of the year it has pinnate leaves, small, purple flowers and black fruits.

❺ Eupatorium purpureum

Joe Pye Weed is a good plant for a large border. It has straight, purple stems with whorls of leaves, and domes of tiny, purplish flowers that attract butterflies.

❻ Sinacalia tanguticus

Nearer the front *Sinacalia* can spread to its heart's content, showing off pretty foliage and plumes of tiny daisy flowers late in the summer.

EXTRA PLANTS TO CONSIDER: *Corylus maxima, Salix exigua, Sambucus* cultivars, maples, birches, *Magnolia demidata, Nothofagus fusca* 'Rainbow'

A QUICK-GROWING BORDER

Sometimes quick-growing plants are required, perhaps to create a screen for privacy, or to fill a gap left after removing a tree or shrub.

Many evergreens are slow growing and a newly planted scheme can look very sparse unless temporarily bulked out with dispensable filling shrubs. Whatever the reason, quick growers can be very useful. Here they are used as a screen across part of a garden.

SOME GROUPS OF *Miscanthus* have been used here to screen views to the landscape beyond. The result gives a walk along the path a sense of mystery, and seems to invite you along to see what is out of view. Quick-growing plants are very useful for all sorts of similar design effects.

SUITABLE SITE: any well-drained soil in sun. *Miscanthus* appreciates added humus

❶ Lavatera 'Candy Floss'

Lavatera is semi-evergreen and soon makes a big bush. The large flowers are produced as the branches grow, giving a long flowering period.

❷ Buddleia davidii 'Black Knight'

The *Buddleia* can reach full size in two or three years. Even if it is hard pruned every year to maintain its arching shape, it will grow back very quickly.

ALTERNATIVE VARIETIES

Lavatera 'Candy Floss'
Lavatera 'Barnsley'
Buddleia davidii 'Black Knight'
Buddleia davidii 'Royal Red'
Macleaya microcarpa
Macleaya microcarpa 'Kelway's Coral Plume'
Helianthus annuus 'Moonwalker'
Any tall annual cultivar
Miscanthus sinensis 'Zebrinus'
Miscanthus sinensis 'Rotsilber'

---

❸ Helianthus annuus 'Moonwalker'

Annuals are wonderfully quick growers, although they obviously only last a season. This is a pretty pale yellow sunflower that grows from about 5 feet (1.5m) up to as much as 15 feet (5m) in good conditions.

❹ Macleaya microcarpa

The perennial *Macleaya* has spreading roots and can reach 7 feet (2m) in a season, making very good screening in the warmer months. It has most attractive foliage, and plumes of buff-colored flowers, tinged with orange.

❺ Miscanthus sinensis 'Zebrinus'

On the end of the bed are a couple of clumps of *Miscanthus*, a tall grass with arching leaves banded with stripes of yellow. Silky flower heads are produced in the fall. The plant can be left through the winter, when its dried foliage and seedheads can look attractive, especially in frosty weather.

EXTRA PLANTS TO CONSIDER: taller cultivars of *Miscanthus, Philadelphus, Salix exigua, Sambucus nigra, Abutilon*

A MISTY LOOK

Gardens on chalk sub-soils are usually free-draining and often hungry, requiring lots of added humus. The plants described here all thrive on dry soils and tolerate alkalinity as long as the fertility is maintained. They are grouped to give a misty look in hazy shades of blue and mauve perennials that seem to go well with the wide horizons of chalk landscapes. There is a succession of flowers from late spring to early fall.

THE FLUFFY FLOWER HEADS of *Thalictrum aquilegifolium* are held above their handsome divided leaves, and give a soft look to any planting. They come in a range of pinks, purples, and white to give gentle color effects. Keep an eye out for powdery mildew in drier conditions, and slugs in wet weather.

SUITABLE SITE: any reasonably fertile soil that is free-draining, especially in winter; tolerant of alkalinity; full sun

ALTERNATIVE VARIETIES

Thalictrum aquilegiifolium
   Thalictrum aquilegiifolium 'Thundercloud'
Dictamnus albus var. purpureus
   Dictamnus albus
Papaver orientale 'Hadspen'
   Papaver orientale 'Blue Moon'
Scabiosa caucasica
   Scabiosa caucasica 'Clive Greaves'
Origanum laevigatum 'Herrenhausen'
   Origanum laevigatum 'Hopleys'
Gypsophila 'Rosenschleier'
   Gypsophila paniculata
   'Flamingo'

❶ Thalictrum aquilegifolium
Meadow rue (*Thalictrum*) is a herbaceous perennial with leaves that resemble a columbine. Fluffy, pale purple flowers appear in early summer, followed by attractive seedheads.

❷ Gypsophila 'Rosenschleier'
Gypsophila is the well-known 'Baby's breath,' with tiny, ball-shaped flowers above lower-growing gray foliage. It prefers to be left undisturbed.

❸ Dictamnus albus var. purpureus
On hot days the volatile oils from the *Dictamnus* can be ignited, giving rise to its common name, burning bush. The flowers are elegant with noticeable stamens.

❹ Papaver orientale 'Hadspen'
This oriental poppy has dusky colored, fragile-looking flowers above rosettes of deeply divided leaves. It dies back after flowering, leaving a hole, but follow Gertrude Jekyll's advice and plant a *Gypsophilla* behind to flop into the gap.

❺ Scabiosa caucasica
Scabiosa caucasica forms clumps of leaves and lots of pale blue flowers. It flowers best after frequent division.

❻ Origanum laevigatum 'Herrenhausen'
At the front of a border the *Origanum* will form mats of leaves with clusters of tall pink flowers in purple bracts later in the season.

EXTRA PLANTS TO CONSIDER: *Stipa calamagrostis, Geranium pratense* 'Mrs. Kendall Clark', *Phuopsis stylosa, Liatris spicata*

The easiest place to experiment with color schemes is in the perennial border. Simple color schemes are very appealing, and the secret of success is to consider flower shape and foliage texture as well as flower color. This combination of pale yellows works all summer, and is unified with the blue annual Nigella damascena *sown directly all around.*

SOFT YELLOWS AND BLUES

A RESTRICTED COLOR THEME can work well if there is a contrast of leaf texture. Here the colors match well, and the filigree leaves of *Coreopsis* in the center look good against the arching *Hemerocallis* leaves to one side and the stiffer, sword-shaped leaves of an iris on the other.

SUITABLE SITE: any good, fertile soil in sun

ALTERNATIVE VARIETIES

Achillea 'Moonshine'
   Achillea 'Taygetea'
Alchemilla mollis
   Alchemilla conjuncta
Anthemis tinctoria 'E C Buxton'
   Anthemis tinctoria var. Kelwayi
Kniphofia 'Little Maid'
   Kniphofia 'Shining Sceptre'
Nigella damascena
   Any blue strain such as
   Nigella 'Miss Jekyll'

Choose cultivars with
similar color to the
plants listed, but
adjust positions
if predicted
heights differ.

❶ *Nigella damascena*
Nigellas are commonly called Love-in-a-Mist thanks to their very finely divided leaves and flower collars. They are hardy annuals, but may self-seed year after year, giving a soft, misty effect to the group, even when the flowers have gone.

❷ *Anthemis tinctoria* 'E C Buxton'
The *Anthemis* has daisy flowers in lemon yellow with a darker center, above mid-green ferny leaves.

❸ *Kniphofia* 'Little Maid'
Edging the front of the group is a small red hot poker, *Kniphofia* 'Little Maid.' It never gets red hot, but remains a cool yellow and green, and flowers well into the fall. The leaves are grass-like and mid green.

❹ *Achillea* 'Moonshine'
Achillea 'Moonshine' has gray-green, finely divided foliage and sulphur-yellow flowers borne in plate-like flower heads, over a long period in the summer. Divide regularly.

❺ *Alchemilla mollis*
Alchemilla mollis is an old favorite, grown as much for its scalloped, almost circular leaves as for its frothy yellow-green flowers. It is very useful for softening edges. If you don't want masses of seedlings, cut off the flowers as they fade.

EXTRA PLANTS TO CONSIDER: *Thalictrum flavum glaveum, Delphinium* 'Butterball'

MAKING AN ENTRANCE

The front door to your home is very important, marking the boundary between the outside world and your private sanctuary. Great care should therefore be taken with the planting, to create a stylish, welcoming look. The first consideration is the type of house. A cottage with roses around the door has always had great appeal, and a restrained planting of clipped evergreens suits a more elegant entrance. It is less obvious how to treat the front door of a modern house. A splash of color is welcoming, and there should be a fair proportion of evergreens to look good all year. A front door is an ideal place to group scented plants to greet people as they come and go.

A WHITE WALL SETS off the dark flowers of a clematis, trained around the doors and windows of a pair of cottages. Roses, hanging baskets and tubs of bedding plants create a charming picture, even where very little garden exists, giving pleasure to visitors and passers-by alike.

SUITABLE SITE: well-drained soils that are moderately fertile and water retentive

❸ *Clematis* 'Perle d'Azur'
Providing a splash of color in the summer, the clematis enjoys having its roots shaded by the *Choisya*, as long as it does not go short of water or food. Give it some form of support that looks attractive when the plant is not in flower.

❹ *Azara serrata*
The *Azara* is evergreen with glossy leaves and fragrant yellow flowers in spring.

❺ *Santolina rosmarinifolia* 'Primrose Gem'
The *Santolina* has a better habit if not well fed, and the clematis likes a lot of added humus. *Santolina* has finely divided, gray, evergreen leaves and button-like yellow flowers. It makes a neat, low dome if not overfed.

❶ *Choisya ternata* 'Sundance'
The yellow of the evergreen *Choisya* is very cheerful, and the leaves are fragrant when crushed. It has white flowers for a long period in summer, starting even earlier in mild climates.

❻ *Salvia officinalis* 'Icterina'
This is a variegated common sage that is handsome enough even without its blue flowers.

❷ *Campanula carpatica*
The ground in front of the shrubs is furnished with a clump-forming campanula. It is low growing and bears lots of blue flowers in summer.

EXTRA PLANTS TO CONSIDER: lavenders, *Pittosporum tenuifolium*, *Piptanthus*, evergreen daphnes

THIS FRONT DOOR HAS been given a symmetrical treatment, with standard bay trees in pots overflowing with bedding, and pots marking the start of the steps. A wisteria has been trained up one side, fronted by sweet rocket. Both will perfume the air to welcome visitors at the door.

AN ELEGANT FRONT DOOR

An elegant approach to a door can be created with a restrained, symmetrical planting. Clipped bay trees in containers are very effective for this and, in cold regions, can be placed away from cold winds and frost. In their absence, tubs of winter interest plants or bulbs could be substituted. In warmer situations the bay trees could be planted directly into the ground. Interesting foliage is useful near a door, as is something to perfume the air. Take into account the paint color of the door when choosing flower colors to plant next to it.

Here the scheme is mostly cool green and white with dashes of color for seasonal interest.

SUITABLE SITE: any fertile, moisture-retaining, yet well-drained soil in partial shade

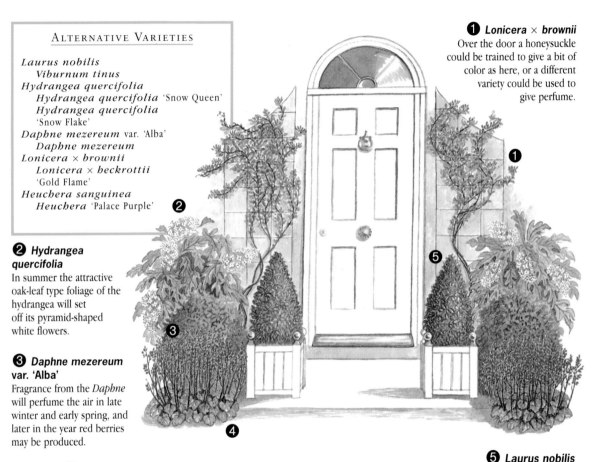

ALTERNATIVE VARIETIES

Laurus nobilis
    Viburnum tinus
Hydrangea quercifolia
    Hydrangea quercifolia 'Snow Queen'
    Hydrangea quercifolia
    'Snow Flake'
Daphne mezereum var. 'Alba'
    Daphne mezereum
Lonicera × *brownii*
    Lonicera × *beckrottii*
    'Gold Flame'
Heuchera sanguinea
    Heuchera 'Palace Purple'

❶ Lonicera × brownii
Over the door a honeysuckle could be trained to give a bit of color as here, or a different variety could be used to give perfume.

❷ Hydrangea quercifolia
In summer the attractive oak-leaf type foliage of the hydrangea will set off its pyramid-shaped white flowers.

❸ Daphne mezereum var. 'Alba'
Fragrance from the *Daphne* will perfume the air in late winter and early spring, and later in the year red berries may be produced.

❹ Heuchera sanguinea
An evergreen edging is provided by the pretty leaves of the heuchera. In summer it has delicate stems bearing many tiny, bell-shaped flowers.

❺ Laurus nobilis
Bays are strong growing and lend themselves to being clipped. Pyramid shapes are the most usual, but you could trim yours to suit yourself, perhaps echoing an architectural feature nearby.

EXTRA PLANTS TO CONSIDER: *Lonicera* × *purpusii, Viburnum tinus, Pieris* cultivars, *Solanum jasminoïdes* 'Album,' *Ajuga reptans, Geranium phaeum* cultivars

VERTICAL GARDENING

There are so many situations where something needs covering with plants that it is fortunate there are so many lovely plants that like to climb.

Walls, fences, sheds, trellises all look better for being clothed in foliage and flowers. Climbing plants can be used on structures to give privacy, or to screen an ugly view. Sometimes a vertical element like an obelisk or rustic tripod is needed to grow plants upwards to give height in an otherwise flat border. Pergolas can give shade and, strategically placed, can provide privacy for seating areas. Here are six climbers that may be used in combination, or singly, according to the size of the support.

A WELL-TRAINED *WISTERIA floribunda* 'Macrobotrys' graces a pergola with its long racemes of fragrant flowers. Pruning a wisteria takes some care, but is well worth the effort.

SUITABLE SITE: fertile, humus-rich, well-drained soil in sun or partial shade

❶ Humulus lupulus 'Aureus'
❷ Clematis 'Niobe'
Another vigorous climber, the golden hop can cover a large structure before dying back each winter. Its lovely sharp, yellow-green leaves are an excellent foil for the deep red flowers of *Clematis* 'Niobe' which can be pruned in late winter when the golden hop is out of the way.

❸ Rosa 'New Dawn'
When the *Wisteria* has finished flowering, the rose 'New Dawn' takes over, with its deep pink buds opening to paler pink.

❹ Passiflora caerulea
Then, in midsummer, the passion flower joins the rose with its intricate flowers borne on almost evergreen foliage.

❺ Wisteria floribunda 'Rosea'
The *Wisteria* looks wonderful on a sturdy pergola, trained so that its long racemes of flowers hang freely down. It is very vigorous and should be grown where it has plenty of room.

❻ Lathyrus latifolius
If any climbers develop bare 'legs,' grow the everlasting sweet pea to disguise them. It is not perfumed like the annual sweet pea, but has bright pink flowers above more substantial leaves.

ALTERNATIVE VARIETIES

Wisteria floribunda 'Rosea'
   Any *Wisteria*
Rosa 'New Dawn'
   Rosa 'Albertine'
Passiflora caerulea
   Passiflora caerulea 'Constance Elliot'
Lathyrus latifolius
   Lathyrus grandiflorus
Humulus lupulus 'Aureus'
   Humulus lupulus 'Taff's Variegated'
Clematis 'Niobe'
   Clematis 'Ville de Lyon'

EXTRA PLANTS TO CONSIDER: climbing roses, *Clematis, Vitis, Hedera, Ampelopsis, Jasminum, Trachelospermum, Holboellia, Bougainvillea, Phaseolus coccineus, Ipomoea hederacea*

City gardens often have higher minimum temperatures than country gardens, allowing a greater range of near-tender plants to be grown. Take advantage of the warmer microclimate and grow these shrubs to

A Sunny Wall in a City Garden

disguise the high walls that can often make a garden seem boxlike and oppressive. If your garden is warm and has a sunny wall, try this combination of plants. They will look even better if the wall is painted white.

THE VARIEGATED LEAVES OF *Actinidia kolomikta* provide plenty of interest, but in early summer it does bear insignificant, fragrant flowers, and female plants may produce ovoid fruits later on. For the best foliage effects, grow it in plenty of sunshine, and choose a spot that is free from strong winds.

SUITABLE SITE: neutral to acid, fertile, well-drained soil in a sheltered, sunny position

❶ *Actinidia kolomikta*
This climber has insignificant flowers, but very showy leaves splashed with pink and white. It looks wonderful on a large, sunny wall where it can develop unconfined.

❷ *Abutilon* × *suntense*
The gray-green leaves of the *Abutilon* are a suitable foil for the saucer-shaped violet flowers. It is fast growing and will soon make a fine show next to the *Actinidia*. Make sure this is kept moist at the roots during summer.

❸ *Elsholtzia stauntonii*
When the *Abutilon* has finished flowering, the *Elsholtzia* will take over, blooming from late summer onwards. It has aromatic leaves that color red in the fall. In colder areas it may die back to ground level in winter.

❹ *Salvia involucrata* 'Bethellii'
At the foot of the *Abutilon*, the *Salvia* also flowers later in the summer with eye-catching flowers borne above aromatic, velvety leaves.

EXTRA PLANTS TO CONSIDER: *Wisteria, Indigofera, Chimonanthus, Nerium oleander, Hibiscus, Ceanothus* 'Marie Simon'

Take advantage of a sheltered spot against a sunny wall and grow something that is at its limit of cold tolerance in

A Sheltered, Sunny Wall

your area. Some walls radiate warmth at night, protecting any plants growing on them. The base of a wall can be very dry, so water and mulch when necessary. These plants need the protection of a warm wall in frost-prone regions, but together they give the feel of somewhere much hotter.

AN IMPOSING WALL DRAPED with *Campsis grandiflora*. The strong red stands up well to the glare of the hot sun, and the heat also encourages it to flower more prolifically.

SUITABLE SITE: any fertile, well-drained soil that is sheltered and sunny all day

❶ Campsis grandiflora
Make sure the *Campsis* has a rich, well-cultivated patch of ground, not too close to the base of the wall. Train it up to the wall and provide permanent support. It only flowers well if sun-baked, but is wonderful when it does.

❸ Coronilla valentina subsp. glauca
Coronilla is an evergreen, dense little bush with lovely scented, pealike flowers that apppear in winter through to the spring, and then at intervals later in the year.

❺ Helianthemum nummularium 'Supreme'
Helianthemum is hardier than the others, but is chosen here for its evergreen, low-growing folige and scarlet flowers. The gryish foliage makes excellent frontal ground cover, and is good foil for all the hot flower colors.

❷ Eucomis bicolor
Eucomis gives a tropical look to the planting, with pineapple-like flowers. It grows from bulbs which appreciate a dry mulch if severe weather is forecast.

❹ Cestrum aurantiacum
Cestrum is an evergreen or semi-evergreen scrambler if left to its own devies, but if you want it under control, it can be cut back to form a rounded shrub. It has yellow orange blooms in summer.

EXTRA PLANTS TO CONSIDER: *Lonicera heckrottii, Callistemon, Buddleia crispa, Crinum, Nerine*

The sun shines on an east wall first thing in the morning and may cause damage to frosted buds and shoots by thawing them too quickly. These plants are tough enough to cope, and have a yellow theme to retain a sunny look all day. There is a contrast in habits and leaf shapes, and a succession of interest through the year. Late flowerers may benefit from the shade of an east wall, and look better for not being scorched by high summer sun.

A Sunny Look for an East Wall

A WONDERFUL CROP OF berries on *Pyracantha rogersiana* 'Flava'. To expose the berries to view it may be necessary to prune away any long new shoots that are produced after flowering. Yellow berries not only look sunny, they are also more likely to be overlooked by birds.

SUITABLE SITE: any reasonable soil in sun or partial shade

❶ *Pyracantha rogersiana flava*

Pyracantha lends itself well to growing on a wall as it can be trimmed to any shape, even around windows. It has white foamy flowers in spring and yellow-orange berries in the fall.

❸ *Jasminum nudiflorum*

This flowers all winter and is trained up to cascade back down. The flowers are useful for picking, and the plain green foliage makes an effective summer backdrop for the plants in front.

❺ Hosta (yellow-leaved cultivars)

In summer, yellow hostas will fill the front of the border with bright leaves. Pale mauve and white flowers stand out against the jasmine. Mulch well to keep growth lush. Yellow hostas color best with some sunshine.

❷ *Hedera colchica* 'Dentata Variegata'

Behind the *Euonymus* the much larger leaves of the ivy make a good contrast. It will need to be encouraged to climb at first, but after a couple of years it will make much better growth.

❹ Euonymus fortunei Emerald 'n' Gold

Evergreen leaves of yellow and green are sometimes tinged with pink in severe weather. It forms a neat mound and may begin to climb an adjacent wall.

❻ Euphorbia griffithii

Euphorbia griffithii is a perennial that prefers partial shade. Its upright stems bear green leaves with red tints. The flower parts are interesting shades of green and orange. The sap can cause skin irritation in some people.

ALTERNATIVE VARIETIES

Pyracantha rogersiana flava
Pyracantha 'Orange Charmer'
Jasminum nudiflorum
Forsythia suspensa
Hedera colchica 'Dentata Variegata'
Hedera colchica 'Sulphur Heart'
Euonymus fortunei Emerald 'n' Gold
Euonymus fortunei 'Sunspot'
Hosta (yellow-leaved cultivar)
Hosta (any yellow cultivars)
Euphorbia griffithii
Euphorbia griffithii 'Fireglow'

EXTRA PLANTS TO CONSIDER: *Clematis, Rosa* 'Madame Alfred Carrière', *Alchemilla mollis* (a good substitute for the hosta if conditions are too shady), *Piptanthus, Kerria japonica*

The way a house sits on the land can be greatly enhanced by the plants grown next to the walls. They can soften the hard angles and stark look of some building materials, but some walls can be open to cold winds, restricting plant choice. Plant a tough shrub in a strategic position to give shelter to other plants nearby.

An Elegant Look for a Shady Wall

A shady wall is valuable for some easily scorched plants. Soil at the foot of a wall can be very dry. Add plenty of humus and water well if dry.

A WALL CLAD WITH *Hydrangea petiolaris* with its flat, lacy flowerheads. It grows to be a large plant, and when grown against a low structure it can look a bit top heavy, but, given enough room, it is a wonderful plant for softening the look of large walls.

SUITABLE SITE: any fertile soil, well-watered, against a shady wall

❶ Hydrangea petiolaris
A bit slow to start, but worth waiting for, this clothes walls with elegant leaves and cream flowers. It is self-clinging and leaves a lacy network of stems in winter.

❷ Viburnum rhytidophyllum
Use the tough *Viburnum rhytidophyllum* to shield other plants from cold winds. It is evergreen with good foliage and cream lacy flowers in spring, followed by black fruits.

❸ Euonymus fortunei 'Silver Queen'
Euonymus fortunei 'Silver Queen' can form a mounded shape or it will happily climb, making it very useful around windows. The green and white of its evergreen leaves will tone in well with the other plants.

ALTERNATIVE VARIETIES

Viburnum rhytidophyllum
    Berberis darwinii
Hydrangea petiolaris
    Pileostegia viburnoïdes
Dicentra spectabilis 'Alba'
    Dicentra (white cultivars)
Cotoneaster salicifolius 'Gnom'
    Cotoneaster conspicuus var. 'Decorus'
Euonymus fortunei 'Silver Queen'
    Hedera helix 'Eva'
Polygonatum × *hybridum*
    Any *Polygonatum* cultivars

❹ Polygonatum × hybridum
The archingstems of Solomon's seal, bear ivory flowers in the late spring. Saw fly larvae may be a problem.

❻ Cotoneaster Salicifolius 'Gnom'
A good horizontal line is provided by the evergreen *Cotoneaster* which will bear cheerful red berries after foamy, white flowers. It makes effective ground cover.

❺ Dicentra spectabilis 'Alba'
At the foot of the dark *Viburnum*, the white flowers of the *Dicentra* will really stand out in early summer.

EXTRA PLANTS TO CONSIDER: *Parthenocissus, Lonicera pileata, Cotoneaster, Euonymus, Tiarella wherryi*

ON TOP OF A WALL

Sunny retaining walls or rocky banks have very dry, often alkaline, soil. By choosing the right plants you can make them look very attractive. It pays to improve the soil as much as possible to give things the best chance of growing well, but there are some plants that thrive in poor, dry soil. Check the pH before planting too; some old walls can be very limey. This collection of plants would look good above a retaining wall, on a rockery, or on a stony bank facing the sun. Remember that trailing plants always grow towards the sun, so if your wall faces away, they will not trail in the direction you might want.

AUBRETIA AND ALYSSUM SAXATILE making their welcome splashes of color on a sunny wall in spring. These mounds have probably been kept neat by being lightly clipped all over right after flowering. This also prevents them from swamping the small alpines in front.

SUITABLE SITE: any neutral to alkaline soil that is very free draining

❶ Scilla peruviana
Scilla peruviana retains its strap-shaped leaves practically all year in warmer climates. It bears big cone-shaped flower heads of purple-blue in early summer.

❷ Phuopsis stylosa
Phuopsis is perennial with leaves that have a starry look. For a long time in summer it is covered in round heads of pink flowers.

❸ Pulsatilla vulgaris
The pasque flower, *Pulsatilla*, is perennial with finely divided leaves covered with tiny, silky hairs. The large, simple flowers in purple are followed by persistent feathery seedheads.

❹ Aubrieta 'Greencourt Purple'
Aubrieta forms dense mats or cascades of gray leaves covered with purple flowers in spring.

❺ Euphorbia myrsinites
Euphorbia myrsinites is a succulent type, with lax stems of gray-green leaves, topped in early summer by lime green flowers. The sap may irritate skin, especially when exposed to sunshine.

❻ Sedum 'Ruby Glow'
This sedum has purple-tinged foliage with a gray bloom, making a good foil for the flattened heads of wine red flowers.

EXTRA PLANTS TO CONSIDER: small hebes, thymes, prostrate rosemary, *Alyssum saxatile*, *Cerastium tomentosum*, *Iberis* cultivars

A
COURTYARD
GARDEN

A sheltered courtyard or warm enclosed garden is a good place to grow plants that would not survive out in the open. It will probably be seen at close quarters all through the year, so grow plants that perform in different seasons. Before buying the plants, make sure that the low winter sun is sufficient to warm the site, and that the soil is well drained. It is often the combination of cold and wet that kills many plants.

FREMONTODENDRON 'CALIFORNIA GLORY' obviously thriving on a sunny wall. The base of the shrub is masked by *Euryops pectinatus*, which has daisy flowers in the same yellow, and pretty grayish foliage. It is not reliably hardy, but will root readily from cuttings.

SUITABLE SITE: well-drained, fertile soil in a warm sheltered site, with full sun

❶ *Fremontodendron* 'California Glory'
This produces showy yellow flowers over a long period in summer. It has scaly leaves and stems that may irritate the skin.

❷ *Acacia pravissima*
The *Acacia* is an arching large shrub or small tree. It has stems well clothed with evergreen, three-sided leaves, and fragrant fluffy yellow flowers in late winter and early spring.

❸ *Rhamnus alaternus* 'Argenteovariegatus'
Rhamnus is also an evergreen with small variegated leaves and yellow-green flowers in early summer. Red berries that turn black are often borne later in the year. It can be clipped to size.

❹ *Ribes laurifolium*
Ribes laurifolium is an evergreen with a low, spreading shape, and yellow-green flowers hanging in clusters in late winter.

❺ *Ceanothus* 'Marie Simon'
The *Ceanothus* has pink flowers in late summer. It is deciduous and may be cut back hard in spring.

❻ *Hibiscus syriacus* 'Mauve Queen'
This *Hibiscus* has large, pale violet flowers with a darker center, carried in late summer and early fall. The shrub is upright and spreading.

EXTRA PLANTS TO CONSIDER: *Zauschneria, Abutilon, Jasminum mesnyi, Clianthus, Indigofera, Grevillea*

PATIO SHRUBS

Patio shrubs need to be undemanding, especially in summer when you want to relax and not look at a lot of plants that need attention. Choose shrubs for the patio area that do something for you, and not the other way round. They should be perfumed or aromatic, have colorful flowers or foliage, and not require much maintenance. Ideally, they should need little pruning or deadheading. They should not be prickly or have sap that irritates the skin.

THIS SEATING AREA IS enclosed by easy care evergreens, highlighted with pots of bedding plants in soft, pastel shades. The muted colors of the furniture, paving, and wall plaques, along with the plant-clothed wall, all contribute to make this patio a relaxing outdoor haven.

Plants around a patio can also be useful, giving shade or shelter from wind, for instance. If you have a barbecue, growing herbs nearby is handy. These shrubs need only a little pruning work in spring.

SUITABLE SITE: well-drained, fertile soil in a sheltered position and plenty of sun

① *Ballota* 'All Hallows Green'

Ballota is evergreen and 'All Hallows Green' has woolly leaves in a shade of green that makes a good foil for the other plants. It has quietly attractive, green flowers, borne in whorls in the leaf axils. It can also be kept neat by cutting to ground level in spring.

② *Helichrysum splendidum*

Helichrysum has silvery foliage with yellow button flowers in summer, but if it is hard pruned in spring it will form a neat dome without any flowers.

③ *Lespedeza thunbergii*

Lespedeza has arching stems bearing trifoliate leaves and many pinky-purple, pea-like flowers in late summer. In cold areas, treat as a perennial and cut down to the ground in winter.

⑤ *Hebe* × *andersonii* 'Variegata'

Hebes are great patio plants. There are many cultivars to choose from, with all sizes, flower colors, and leaf types. Choose one to suit your patio. This one is more tender than the plain-leaved type, but the leaves are attractively variegated and show off the purple flowers.

> ### ALTERNATIVE VARIETIES
>
> *Helichrysum splendidum*
> *Helichrysum italicum*
> *Indigofera kirilowii*
> *Indigofera heterantha*
> *Indigofera decora*
> *Hebe* × *andersonii* 'Variegata'
> *Hebe* (many summer-flowering cultivars)
> *Lespedeza thunbergii*
> *Lespedeza bicolor*
> *Rosmarinus officinalis* 'Albus'
> *Rosmarinus officinalis* and cultivars
> *Ballota* 'All Hallows Green'
> *Ballota pseudodictamnus*
> *Ballota italica*

④ *Rosmarinus officinalis* 'Albus'

Rosemary is lovely on a patio if you cook on a barbecue. It can be used for flavoring, and twigs thrown on the flames scent the air. This one has white flowers and is quite tender, but any rosemary would do.

⑥ *Indigofera kirilowii*

Indigofera will spread at the roots to make good ground cover. It has pretty leaves, giving a ferny effect, and clusters of rose-pink flowers in summer. Cut to ground level in spring to obtain fresh foliage in summer.

EXTRA PLANTS TO CONSIDER: *Potentilla* cultivars, *Salvia officinalis* and cultivars, oregano, bay, fuchsia, *Hydrangea macrophylla* and cultivars

A patio or seating area is for you to sit and relax, so surround it with easy-care perennials that flower for long periods. Good patio plants should not need staking, tying in, or deadheading, and should provide color, perfume, or foliage interest during the summer months.

Prepare the soil well before planting, and if the site is in a hot spot, choose drought-tolerant plants, or install irrigation. The last thing you want to do in your leisure time is lug watering cans to rescue wilting plants.

EASY PERENNIALS FOR A PATIO

A *PENSTEMON* DEMONSTRATING HOW useful they are for easy summer color. Deadheading helps to keep them flowering vigorously, and it pays to take softwood cuttings to guard against loss in extreme weather, but otherwise they are not demanding. Here *Penstemon* 'Ruby' is teamed with the more tender *Felicia capensis* 'Santa Anna'.

SUITABLE SITE: well-drained, fertile soil in sun

❶ Achillea 'Appleblossom'
Achilleas have flat flower heads that contrast well with vertical flowers. This variety comes in shades of pink, but there are many yellow forms too.

❷ Salvia × superba
The *Salvia* has bushy, mid-green foliage and upright blue flowers with purple bracts in summer and early fall.

❸ Acanthus spinosus
Acanthus is a perennial of architectural presence, with a mound of large leaves, deeply cut and shiny. It has imposing spires of hooded flowers in white with purple bracts during early summer. It self seeds, but unwanted seedlings can be pulled out in spring.

❺ Oenothera speciosa 'Rosea'
The spreading nature of this evening primrose may be useful near a patio, or hard surface, as it can fill up empty patches of soil. Be careful, though, as it can be invasive if given free reign. In spite of its name, the flowers do open in the daytime, revealing white and pink flowers with deep pink veining. They are very fragrant.

❹ Penstemon 'Alice Hindley'
This is a long-flowering plant that comes in many colors. In mild climates, the hardier ones are evergreen. This one has violet tubular, flared flowers.

❻ Veronica austriaca subsp. teucrium
This carpet-forming *veronica* has gray-green leaves with narrow spikes of vivid blue flowers in early summer.

EXTRA PLANTS TO CONSIDER: Aster, Anthemis punctata subsp. cupaniana, Erigeron, Geranium, Diascia, Physostegia, Eryngium, Echinops, Cerastium tomentosum, Agapanthus, Gazania

AN INFORMAL GRAVEL PATH

A gravel path can be given a wonderfully informal look by planting either side with spreading or self-seeding plants and then mulching around them with more gravel. In that way the plants colonize the path, blurring the edges and softening them. A gravel mulch has other benefits too. It slows evaporation, keeping soils more moist, and it reflects sunlight, warming the shoots and leaves. Thus, in a warm, sunny spot, plants of borderline hardiness can be successfully grown. These plants have been chosen to give interesting foliage contrasts.

GRAVEL HAS BEEN SUPPLEMENTED here with larger rocks and stones to give the effect of a dry riverbed. The plants have been placed to enhance the effect, with planting becoming more dense up the banks. Spikes are provided by grasses and the dark *Phomium tenax* 'Bronze Baby'.

SUITABLE SITE: any well-drained, or even dry, soil in sun

ALTERNATIVE VARIETIES

Verbascum bombyciferum
    Verbascum chaixii 'Gainsborough'
Centranthus ruber
    None, but self-seeds freely
Phormium 'Dazzler'
    Phormium colensoi 'Maori Queen'
Sedum spectabile subsp. *maximum* 'Atropurpureum'
    Sedum 'Ruby Glow'
Eryngium alpinum
    Eryngium × *zabelii*
Osteospermum ecklonii
    Osteospermum jucundum

❶ *Eryngium alpinum*
Maritime *Eryngium* naturally grows on shingle, so it looks well in gravel. Jagged-edged leaves and wiry blue stems bear blue flower heads with spiny collars.

❷ *Sedum telephium* subsp. *maximum* 'Atropurpureum'
This sedum has dark red-purple, fleshy leaves with a white bloom. Its lax stems carry masses of starry, little flowers. It tolerates dry conditions, and the leaves contrast well with the gravel.

❸ *Phormium* 'Dazzler'
The upright leaves of this red flax are a strong architectural feature. Its evergreen leaves have red stripes. Mature plants send up tall flowers.

❹ *Verbascum bombyciferum*
A tall biennial, or short-lived perennial, this self seeds all around. It has imposing spires of yellow flowers, and silvery-white woolly stems and leaves.

❺ *Centranthus ruber*
Red valerian has fleshy, gray leaves and cone-shaped flower heads in shades of red and pink. It thrives in dry stony spots, and self seeds.

❻ *Osteospermum ecklonii*
This is a prostrate plant that spreads steadily over gravel. The blue-gray flowers open in bright sunlight to reveal blue-centered, white flowers, which age to pink.

EXTRA PLANTS TO CONSIDER: *Gypsophila, Alchemilla, Artemisia, Salvia, Hebe, Acaena*

THE FROTHY FLOWERS OF *Alchemilla mollis* repeated along the edges of this double herbaceous border give unity and soften the look of the very straight path. The color of the flowers is useful for toning down, or separating, more difficult flower colors. *Stachys* performs the same function in the foreground.

BORDER-FRONT PERENNIALS

Low-growing plants play an important role at the front of borders where they soften edges, suppress weeds and perhaps hide unattractive bases of taller plants behind. If they are evergreen, so much the better for winter interest. Late-emerging frontal perennials are also useful for disguising the fading foliage of spring bulbs and corms.

Try not to make all edging plants prostrate; vary the height a little to give a more interesting effect.

SUITABLE SITE: the front of any border on reasonably fertile soil that is not too dry, in sun or partial shade

❶ Stachys macrantha 'Superba'

Stachys macrantha is not evergreen, but in summer the crinkly leaves make effective weed-smothering ground cover. Pink and purple flower spikes appear for a long time in late summer.

❷ Persicaria affinis

Persicaria is only semi-evergreen, but the leaves remain on the plant making an attractive toffee-colored mat of foliage all winter. The pink and red flower spikes are produced all summer.

ALTERNATIVE VARIETIES

Vinca minor 'Argenteovariegata'
   Vinca minor cultivars
Ophiopogon planiscapus 'Nigrescens'
   Liriope muscari
Persicaria affinis
   Persicaria filiformis cultivars
Stachys macrantha 'Superba'
   Stachys macrantha 'Robusta'
Erigeron 'Charity'
   Erigeron 'Dimity'
Ajuga reptans 'Burgundy Glow'
   Ajuga reptans 'Multicolor'

---

❺ Ophiopogon planiscapus 'Nigrescens'

Ophiopogon is an evergreen perennial with arching, grass-like leaves in a dusky purple-black. It has small pale violet flowers, and makes good ground cover.

❸ Erigeron 'Charity'

This *Erigeron* forms low clumps of leaves bearing many daisy-like flowers with pink rays and yellow centers. It is in bloom from early to late summer.

❹ Vinca minor 'Argenteovariegata'

Vinca is an evergreen sub-shrub with long stems that root when they contact the ground, making effective ground cover. It can be kept in check by shearing over in spring. Blue periwinkle flowers are borne above variegated foliage for a long period in spring and early summer.

❻ Ajuga reptans 'Burgundy Glow'

Ajuga makes great carpets as long as the soil is not too dry. It is evergreen and has silvery leaves suffused with wine red. It may be scorched by very hot sun.

EXTRA PLANTS TO CONSIDER: *Alchemilla, Aubretia, Cerastium, Liriope spicata, Phlox subulata, Sedum*

A BED OF ROSES

A well-planned rose garden is a wonderful place, with a succession of blooms of different shapes and perfumes from spring to fall. There are roses of all sizes and habits so no garden need be without.

Roses need to be fed and mulched regularly. On light or free-draining soils, do whatever you can to improve the ground before planting. Keep roses watered in dry weather—about 1in (25mm) of water each week—so they can take up nutrients from the soil.

The roses in this scheme are all in shades of pink, but with contrasting habits to show how varied they can be.

THIS PRETTY WOODEN ARCH provides the perfect support for a pink rose. A perfumed rose with this many blooms would be wonderful to walk under. The rose in the picture has been well grown and trained, with good, busy growth right from the base, and plenty of healthy leaves and flowers.

SUITABLE SITE: enriched soil in sun

❶ *Rosa* 'Kew Rambler'
Vigorous enough to grow over an arch or pergola, this climber has good grayish leaves and plentiful wild rose-type flowers. It has a powerful fragrance and small orange hips. It is pictured here growing over an arch, but it would also be lovely on a bower with seating underneath.

❸ *Rosa* Queen Elizabeth
Queen Elizabeth is a strong-growing, upright rose suitable for the back of a border, or as a specimen. It has good foliage and lovely blooms that last well when cut for flower arranging.

❷ *Rosa* 'The Fairy'
At the front of the group is 'The Fairy,' an old-fashioned looking rose that makes good ground cover in front of taller types. It is late to begin flowering, but then flowers continuously for weeks.

❹ *Rosa* Brother Cadfael
Brother Cadfael is a bushy rose with huge, peony-like flowers with a rich fragrance.

EXTRA PLANTS TO CONSIDER: *Rosa* 'Cottage Rose', *Rosa* 'Bonica', *Rosa* 'Zepherine Drouhin'

Roses look lovely planted in company with other perennials at the front of the border. They help to keep down weeds and disguise the manured earth around the bases of the roses. The end result is so much better than the municipal rose bed look, which has

PERENNIALS

FOR A

ROSE BED

gaunt roses set in expanses of bare soil. There are many perennials to choose from; these are mainly in soft shades that won't compete with the roses. Low-growing, gray foliage plants would also look good.

'ARTHUR BELL' IS THE yellow rose in this bed, set off simply and most effectively by *Campanula portenschlagiana*. In comparison, the red rose looks gangly and lonely against almost bare soil. The *Campanula* may become too much of a good thing, though, and may need checking from time to time.

SUITABLE SITE: these all prefer a well-drained, fertile soil in sun

❶ *Nepeta* × *faassenii*

Soft gray-green aromatic foliage with pale blue flowers of the catmint *Nepeta* look lovely sprawling on a path in front of roses. Bees love the flowers, as do cats. Cut it back hard for a second flush later in the summer.

❷ *Diascia* 'Ruby Field'

Diascia has upright little flowers of apricot pink. It forms a low mat of leaves suitable for the front of a border, and blooms from midsummer well into the fall.

ALTERNATIVE VARIETIES

Nepeta × *faassenii*
    Nepeta 'Six Hills Giant'
Geranium endressii
    Geranium 'Wargrave Pink'
Alchemilla mollis
    Alchemilla conjuncta
Diascia 'Ruby Field'
    Diascia rigescens
Lavandula angustifolia 'Hidcote'
    Lavandula angustifolia 'Munstead'

❸ *Geranium endressii*

The herbaceous geranium has leaves of contrasting shape, and simple pink flowers produced over a long period.

❹ *Alchemilla mollis*

Alchemilla mollis seems to belong with roses. It has scallop-edged, almost circular leaves which hold drops of water like jewels. Some people cut off the pale lime-green flowers to prevent self-seeding, but they look too pretty to waste.

❺ *Lavandula angustifolia* 'Hidcote'

Lavenders and roses also seem to belong together, although the lavender does not need feeding as much as the roses. The mounds of evergreen grayish foliage are excellent for disguising the feet of roses behind. The flowers add their perfume to those of the roses.

EXTRA PLANTS TO CONSIDER: low-growing *Artemisia*, *Campanula*, *Stachys byzantina*, *Veronica* cultivars, *Ageratum*

COTTAGE GARDEN PERENNIALS

The essential characteristics of a cottage garden are informality and abundance. The actual choice of plants is not as important as how they are arranged. The borders should be filled with plants of all sorts and sizes, with no obvious attempt to color coordinate them.

The plants should look as though they have self seeded and grown where they liked. Along with roses, honeysuckle, lavender, pinks, and herbs of all sorts, try these perennials. Grow the taller ones nearest to the back, and the shorter ones toward the front, but never too obviously arranged.

A RIOT OF DELPHINIUMS, roses and other perennials gives a relaxed cottage garden look to this border. The foxgloves are biennial or short-lived perennials, but self seed about the garden in varying colors. Penstemons, such as the ones in the foreground, are also reliable perennials for this type of garden.

SUITABLE SITE: moisture-retentive, but well-drained soil, and there should be sun for a good part of the day

❶ Rudbeckia laciniatus
Also a tall plant, the
Rudbeckia has daisy flowers
with a green central cone.

❷ Lysimachia punctata
Lysimachia punctata has a cottagey
look with its upright stems of green
leaves and yellow flowers. It is prone
to spread in very moist conditions,
but in a normal soil it is
well behaved.

❸ Galega 'Duchess of Bedford'
Galega, or goat's rue, is
a large plant that needs
support for its divided
leaves and pea-like
flowers.

❹ Echinops ritro
Echinops ritro has
jagged-edged leaves, and tall
stems bearing steely blue globe
flowers that are good for drying
if picked before the seed sets.

❺ Achillea 'Coronation Gold'
The familiar flat flower heads of *Achillea*
are a good contrast to the other flowers,
and the leaves are finely divided and ferny.

❻ Geum chiloense 'Fire Opal'
At the lowest level is the fiery
orange of the *Geum*. It has
mounds of green leaves with
clusters of double blooms.

EXTRA PLANTS TO CONSIDER: *Alchemilla mollis*, *Nepeta* cultivars, *Astrantia* cultivars, *Sidalcea* cultivars, *Acanthus*

AN ENGLISH-STYLE HERBACEOUS BORDER

Traditional herbaceous borders have a timeless appeal, and this one has all the right ingredients to recreate the look. The taller plants will need support, but do not leave staking until the plants begin to topple. They will not recover their poise. As soon as the shoots are above ground, put in twiggy sticks, circles of canes and string, or special plant supports. If you adjust the heights as the plants grow, the supports need not be visible when the plants are in flower.

GROUPS OF PERENNIALS ARE arranged by height and color to give a traditional look. Where there were gaps in the border, some tender bedding plants have been used to fill in. This can be done throughout the season to ring the changes and experiment with color and form.

SUITABLE SITE: humus-rich, well-drained, fertile soil in sun

❶ *Paeonia lactiflora* 'Baroness Schröder'
The peony has reddish shoots in spring, and attractive divided foliage that colors up in the fall. The flowers are large, fully double, white and blush pink. Don't lift and divide with the other perennials as peonies resent disturbance.

❷ *Delphinium* 'Centurion Blue Sky'
The vital ingredient in a traditional herbaceous border, the Delphiniums are well worth a bit of effort with staking and with pampering. Their tall blue spires can be cut back before they go to seed, to encourage further flowering.

❸ *Phlox paniculata* 'Eva Cullum'
Phlox paniculata is an old favorite, with big, perfumed flower heads. Grow plenty, as they are good for cutting. 'Eva Cullum' is bright pink with a deeper eye, but there are plenty of other colors to choose from.

ALTERNATIVE VARIETIES

Delphinium 'Centurion Blue Sky'
   Any tall blue cultivar
Sidalcea 'Elsie Heugh'
   Any *Sidalcea* or *Alcea*
Phlox paniculata 'Eva Cullum'
   Phlox paniculata cultivars
Paeonia lactiflora 'Baroness Schröder'
   Paeonia lactiflora 'Sarah Bernhardt' or similar
Geranium endressii
   Geranium 'Wargrave Pink'

❹ *Geranium endressii*
A line of geranium edges the front of the border, with its pretty leaves and simple, pink flowers. Cut back hard if it grows too lax, and it will soon grow back again.

❺ *Sidalcea* 'Elsie Heugh'
Sidalcea is a hollyhock look-alike, but not so tall or prone to rust. It does not relish a very alkaline soil.

EXTRA PLANTS TO CONSIDER: lupins, *Sedum* cultivars, *Salvia* cultivars, *Alcea*, *Lilium*, *Alchemilla mollis*

A Shady Border on Acid Soil

The calm of a natural woodland can be created, even in a small garden, by choosing the right sort of plants. You need to remember that in natural deciduous woodlands, the annual fall of leaves creates a deep, moisture-retentive litter which supports a range of plants that need this type of soil, as well as the light conditions created by deciduous trees. If you have well-drained, acid soil and a site in partial shade, or can replicate it by adding humus, then this grouping of plants will have year-round appeal, and bring the woodland feel to your backdoor.

HAMAMELIS × INTERMEDIA 'Ruby Glow' sheds its vibrantly colored autumn leaves to give a carpet of color against a background of somber evergreens. A real two-season plant, it is also invaluable for its spidery flowers, which scent the air even in the bleakest months.

SUITABLE SITE: partially shaded border with well-drained, acid soil

❶ Fothergilla major
Fothergilla has fragrant flowers in spring when clusters of stamens decorate the new leaves. It has reliable fall leaf color too.

❷ Hamamelis × intermedia 'Pallida'
The *Hamamelis*, or witch hazel, has a wide, spreading shape and fragrant spidery flowers, even in the coldest weather. Its leaves turn buttery yellow before falling, giving it another season of interest.

❸ Desfontainia spinosa 'Harold Comber'
Desfontainia is an evergreen, upright shrub with handsome, prickly foliage and yellowy red tubular flowers in the fall. It may be slow to grow, but worth the wait.

❹ Trillium sessile
This is a handsome woodland perennial that puts on a show at a lower level in spring, with its maroon spotted leaves and deep red flowers in spring.

❺ Kirengeshoma palmata
Late in summer pale yellow flowers bloom on dark stems above sycamore-like leaves. Needs a sheltered spot and protection from slugs.

❻ Callicarpa bodinieri var. giraldii 'Profusion'
A bushy and upright plant. Pink summer flowers are followed by violet fruit in fall. They bear more fruit if planted in groups.

EXTRA PLANTS TO CONSIDER: *Pieris* cultivars, *Daphne* × *burkwoodii*, *Corylopsis* cultivars, *Primula* cultivars

A Scheme for Dry Shade

In many gardens there are shady patches of ground where nothing seems to grow well. Usually they are near hungry trees or hedges, or in shady corners near a building where little rain can reach. The plants in this plan will tolerate dry shade and even thrive if given the right sort of attention while they become established. This scheme of yellows and greens will relieve the gloom and, once established, will not involve much maintenance.

Aucuba japonica brings a sunny look to a shady site. These are very accommodating shrubs that grow in all but waterlogged situations. They are invaluable for evergreen leaves in dry shade, and are good for hedging, as in this picture where Busy Lizzies have been added for a splash of color.

SUITABLE SITE: any shady situation, even with dry soil

❶ *Aucuba japonica* '**Crotonifolia**'

Aucuba, or spotted laurels, are forgiving shrubs that brighten all sorts of unpromising situations. This one will eventually make a dome of yellow-splashed leaves, bringing a bit of light to the gloom. Give it a good start with humus-enriched soil, and water well in dry spells. The plain-leaved form 'Rozannie' is just as handsome, and tolerates even deeper shade.

❷ *Sarcococca confusa*

Sarcococcas are quiet but valuable little evergreens that cover the ground and scent the air all around in winter.

❸ *Iris foetidissima*

Foliage contrast is provided by the *Iris foetidissima* which has tough, sword-shaped leaves. The flowers are not important, but are followed by pods that split to reveal red berries in winter.

❹ *Symphoricarpos albus*

Symphoricarpos will do sterling work too in the same conditions, spreading steadily to give good ground cover, but the white berries will not be so prolific in deep shade.

❺ *Euphorbia amygdaloïdes* subsp. *robbiae*

Euphorbia robbiae is also good ground cover, and has long-lasting flower heads of lime green in spring.

❻ *Vinca minor* '**Aureovariegata**'

Vinca minor has low, trailing shoots that root where they contact soil, making weed-suppressing mats of gold-edged leaves. Purple periwinkle flowers appear in spring.

EXTRA PLANTS TO CONSIDER: *Mahonia, Ruscus, Ribes sanguineum, Epimedium, Lamium, Alchemilla, Cyclamen, Clivia miniata*

These few plants will produce flowers for weeks on end, stretching the summer right into late fall. They are

LONG-FLOWERING PLANTS FOR PARTIAL SHADE

tolerant plants, blooming in partial shade, and only needing a minimum amount of maintenance. The soil should be moisture-retentive but well-drained, acid, or alkaline.

WARNING: Aconitum is deadly poisonous if eaten.

THIS MOP-HEAD HYDRANGEA, growing against a shady house wall, provides plenty of interest over a long period for this path around the house. If this were a dry, as well as shady situation, it would be a good idea to use a soaker hose, or install an automatic watering system to keep the hydrangea well watered.

SUITABLE SITE: any reasonable soil in sun or partial shade

❶ Hydrangea macrophylla

Hydrangea macrophylla comes in lacecap or mophead types, and flower color can be affected by soil pH. In acid soils they tend toward blues and purples, on alkaline soils they are more pink or red. They are good for cutting and drying, and their faded flower heads remain attractive right into winter.

❷ Fuchsia magellanica

The *Fuchsia* is hardy in some areas (check directory for details), and will regrow from the base if damaged by frost. Plant deeply and provide a thick layer of mulch to protect it in very cold weather.

> ### ALTERNATIVE VARIETIES
>
> *Fuchsia magellanica*
>   *Fuchsia* 'Riccartonii,' *Fuchsia magellanica* var. *gracilis*
> *Hydrangea macrophylla*
>   Any mophead or lacecap cultivar
> *Hypericum* 'Hidcote'
>   *Hypericum* 'Rowallane'
> *Aconitum* 'Newry Blue'
>   *Aconitum* 'Sparks Variety,' 'Bressingham Spire'
>   *Anemone* × *hybrida* cultivars

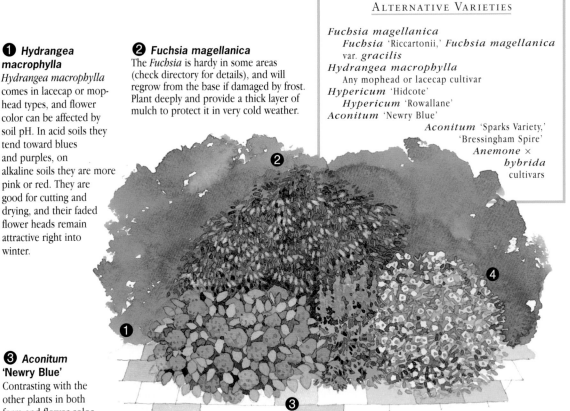

❸ Aconitum 'Newry Blue'

Contrasting with the other plants in both form and flower color, the *Aconitum* is a tall blue flowering plant with handsome divided leaves. It is fatally poisonous if eaten. If there is any risk of accidental ingestion, for example, by a child or pet, substitute this plant with an *Anemone hupehensis* cultivar.

❹ Hypericum 'Hidcote'

The *Hypericum* is a tough little plant, evergreen except in severe weather. Cheerful yellow flowers are borne from early summer to late fall.

EXTRA PLANTS TO CONSIDER: *Schizophragma hydrangeoïdes, Lathyrus latifolius, Lonicera periclymenum* 'Serotina,' *Tricyrtis hirta,* evergreen azaleas, hellebores

WHO COULD RESIST THE colors of rhododendrons in a woodland setting? Here they have been planted in graded heights to lead the eye to the soaring trunks of silver birch and conifers. The woodland floor is carpeted with ferns and low-growing perennials to complete the look.

A WOODLAND EDGE

If you have some tall trees, or a similar shaded site and want to plant some rhododendrons for their wonderful spring color, but don't want the static look that sometimes comes from mass plantings of the hybrid types, then try adding plants with contrasting forms and flowering times.

There are literally hundreds of rhododendrons to choose from. Pick ones to suit your taste and the space available.

SUITABLE SITE: humus-rich, moist, acid soil in partial shade

❸ *Pleioblastus auricoma*

A bit of rustling movement among the evergreens comes from the bamboo, *Pleioblastus auricoma*. The bright foliage and canes are a welcome contrast in form as well as color.

❹ *Rhododendron austrinum* 'Betty'
❺ *Rhododendron austrinum* 'Seta'

There are many rhododendrons to choose, so make a personal choice, based on the time of flowering, leaf type, and eventual height. The suggestions here were chosen to fit well with the other shrubs and to give a succession of flower color. 'Seta' blooms early and can grow to 3–5ft (1–1.5m), and 'Betty' blooms later. When not in bloom the bushes give an attractive undulating edge to the group.

---

❶ *Hydrangea paniculata* 'Unique'

Late summer flowers are provided by the hydrangea with its extra large blooms in creamy white which illuminate the shade. It can grow quite tall, so prune to a framework each spring once established.

❷ *Kalmia latifolia* 'Ostbo Red'

Kalmia is a large, evergreen shrub ideal as a background for the light flowers and leaves of the other shrubs. 'Ostbo Red' has dark buds opening to paler pink flowers in spring.

ALTERNATIVE VARIETIES

Kalmia latifolia 'Ostbo Red'
  Kalmia latifolia cultivars
Hydrangea paniculata 'Unique'
  paniculata cultivars, or *Hydrangea quercifolia*
Rhododendron austrinum 'Seta'
  Any similar sized cultivars
Rhododendron austrinum 'Betty'
  Any similar sized cultivars
Pleioblastus auricomus
  Pleioblastus viridistriatus, or similar (but beware invasive cultivars)

EXTRA PLANTS TO CONSIDER: *Pieris, Camellias, Acer* species, *Fothergilla, Corylopsis pauciflora, Hosta, Rodgersia*

WOODLAND
PERENNIALS

Between deciduous trees or tall shrubs, grow some perennials to create a woodland glade effect. Early in the year is the time most woodland plants flower, before the shade from the tree canopy becomes too dense, but foxgloves may go on blooming until midsummer. As long as the soil is moisture retentive, rich in humus, but well drained, these plants will grow happily in shade or sun.

Left to their own devices, they may even become naturalized.

A NATURAL-LOOKING woodland planting, with *Anemone nemorosa* at the foot of some pale-flowered rhododendrons. Further interest at ground level along the path is provided by violets, trillium, celandine, and cyclamen. The natural look is preserved by the use of bark for the path.

SUITABLE SITE: any humus-rich soil beneath deciduous shrubs or trees

❶ *Meconopsis cambrica*
Welsh poppies can be a nuisance because they self seed. In this setting that is part of their charm. Slender stems bear yellow or orange poppies in late spring.

❷ *Digitalis ferruginea*
Although this foxglove is short-lived, it is still worth growing and may naturalize. It has basal rosettes of coarse leaves and tall spikes of soft apricot blooms.

ALTERNATIVE VARIETIES

Ranunculus ficaria 'Brazen Hussy'
    Ranunculus ficaria cultivars
Epimedium × *versiedor* 'Sulphareum'
Primula vulgaris subsp. *sibthorpii*
    Primula vulgaris
Meconopsis cambrica
    Meconopsis cambrica flore pleno
Anemone sylvestris
    Anemone nemorosa
Aquilegia vulgaris
    Aquilegia vulgaris cultivars
Digitalis ferruginea
    Digitalis grandiflora

❻ *Anemone sylvestris*
Following the primroses come the wood anemones. This type has spreading roots and the usual jagged-edged leaves. The delicate-looking white flowers enliven the shade beneath trees.

❸ *Primula vulgaris* subsp. *sibthorpii*
Primroses are the essence of early spring. This one has a pale lilac tinge to the petals and a greenish-yellow eye.

❹ *Ranunculus ficaria* 'Brazen Hussy'
In early spring this bronze-leaved lesser celandine makes spreading mats of heart-shaped leaves, with bright golden-yellow flowers. The foliage dies away before summer.

❺ *Aquilegia vulgaris*
Aquilegia vulgaris seed themselves, giving rise to varying flower colors. The foliage is prettily divided and looks a bit like maidenhair fern.

EXTRA PLANTS TO CONSIDER: bluebells, *Epimedium, Asperula odorata, Lamium, Pulmonaria, Ajuga,* candelabra primulas, *Arthropodium cirrhatum*

A LUSH WOODLAND-STREAM LOOK

The atmosphere of the woodland stream is one of shady calm, with growth so luxuriant you can almost hear it above the sound of the water.

HOSTAS, IRIS, PRIMULAS, AND a bold, central clump of *Peltiphyllum peltatum* crowd the banks of this tiny stream to create a picture of foliage contrasts, although there are flowers besides the primula at other times. The seat and mossy rocks are almost hidden by lush growth.

If you have a moist-to-boggy site with partial shade, try these plants to recreate that atmosphere in your garden. The leaves are bold and dramatic so try to avoid sites prone to wind that may damage them, or provide a sheltering screen on the windward side. Sunlight would be fine, especially if dappled, but harsh midday sun would dry out the soil too much.

SUITABLE SITE: fertile, moist-to-boggy soil that does not dry out, and a sheltered site in partial shade

ALTERNATIVE VARIETIES

Gunnera manicata
   Gunnera tinctoria
Lysichiton americanus
   Zantedeschia aethiopica cultivars
Filipendula rubra 'Venusta'
   Filipendula rubra. and cultivars
Pleioblastus auricomus
   Typha minima
Ligularia dentata 'Desdemona'
   Ligularia dentata 'Othello,' 'The Rocket'
Inula magnifica
   Inula hookeri

❶ *Ligularia dentata* 'Desdemona'

This *Ligularia* has rounded leaves of a brown tint with deep maroon undersides. The mid to late summer flowers are a deep orange color.

❷ *Filipendula rubra* 'Venusta'

Filipendula is vigorous and spreading with jagged-edged leaves and plumes of feathery pink flowers. There are smaller cultivars for a more restricted site.

❸ *Gunnera manicata*

Gunnera is a highly architectural plant, with huge leaves with serrated edges and prickly stems. Conical pink flowers appear in early summer.

❹ *Lysichiton americanus*

Lysichiton produces its giant arum flowers in early spring. It gives off a slightly unpleasant smell, so site it away from the house.

❺ *Inula magnifica*

Inula magnifica is large enough to go well with *Gunnera*. It has broad leaves and a spreading habit. In late summer it puts out furry buds opening to yellow daisies.

❻ *Pleioblastus auricomus*

The bamboo spreads at the roots and has leaves broadly striped in yellow and green, although in deeper shade the striping is not so marked. It provides an upright, airy accent in the grouping.

EXTRA PLANTS TO CONSIDER: *Trollius, Symphytum, Peltiphyllum peltatum, Botumus, Iris laevigata*

A PONDSIDE PLANTING

Part of the art of siting a pond in a garden involves sympathetic planting around it. The most straightforward way is to choose plants (and their cultivars) that prefer wet or moist soil conditions, and then group them to enhance the style of pond. Strong shapes and outlines reflected in still water look effective, as do plants that arch over the water surface. Pond edgings can be disguised by foliage if necessary. This pond is planted with flowering plants that soften the hard lines and rectangular shape, yet they do not pretend to be too "natural" looking. Their peak flowering time is late summer to fall.

CONTRASTING FORMS AND TEXTURES characterize this quiet pondside planting. The pale flowers of the feathery astilbe, and the tall iris are complemented by the nearby white-striped leaves. The horizontal line of the rock is well placed at the foot of the vertical iris leaves.

SUITABLE SITE: moist, humus-rich soil that does not dry out in summer. Sun or partial shade

ALTERNATIVE VARIETIES

Sanguisorba obtusa
    Filipendula purpurea
Dierama pulcherrimum
    Dierama 'Miranda'
Lythrum salicaria 'Firecandle'
    Lythrum salicaria 'Robert'
Chelone obliqua
    Chelone obliqua var. *alba*
Cimicifuga simplex Atropurpurea
    Group
    Cimicifuga simplex 'Brunette',
    'Elstead'
Astilbe chinensis var. *pumila*
    Astilbe 'Sprite',
    'Serenade'

❷ Dierama pulcherrimum
Dierama is also known as "angel's fishing rod" because of its fine, arching stems that have open pink bell flowers delicately hung at the ends. It looks lovely next to still water.

❶ Cimicifuga simplex Atropurpurea Group
Cimicifuga has long, thin, often curved spires of flower heads on wiry stems. They look full of movement. This form has tones of pink and purple.

❹ Lythrum salicaria 'Firecandle'
Lythrum will grow in an ordinary border too, but its strong upright habit looks especially good near water. Spikes of rich pink appear in late summer, and in some years the foliage may color up in the fall.

❸ Sanguisorba obtusa
Sanguisorba has attractive blue-green leaves and fluffy rose-pink flowers. It may need a few twiggy sticks for support.

❺ Chelone obliqua
Chelone has an upright habit, with hooded flowers giving rise to its common name, "Turtle Head." The stems are well clothed with dark green leaves.

❻ Astilbe chinensis var. pumila
Astilbes have creeping roots and are ideal for clothing pond edges. They have deeply divided leaves and loose flower heads in late summer.

EXTRA PLANTS TO CONSIDER: *Astilboïdes, Filipendula, Aruncus, Astrantia, Lobelia fulgens, Rodgersia, Hosta, Ajuga, Houttuynia,* candelabra primulas

Wildflower meadows look beautiful, but can be difficult to establish. Annual wildflowers tend to die out in

PERENNIALS TO NATURALIZE IN GRASS

permanent grass, so use perennials that can cope with the competition from unmown grass. You may have to experiment a little to find plants that suit your soil and climate, but these are good to try for a start. Remove some turf from around the planting holes to reduce competition while they become established. Mow in late summer, and then a couple more times before the winter, to start the next growing season with short grass.

DIFFERENT COLORS AND HEIGHTS harmonize to create the atmosphere of high summer in a wild meadow. The choice of plants is not as important as their massed effect, and ability to thrive in long grass with minimum maintenance.

SUITABLE SITE: soil that is well drained, not too rich, and in full sun

❶ Gladiolus communis subsp. *byzantinus*
This species *Gladiolus* has stiff sword-shaped leaves and magenta flowers. It will increase steadily if happy.

❷ Echinacea purpurea 'Robert Bloom'
Echinacea, or Cone-flower, has upright stems of daisy-like flowers, each with an orange-brown, raised center. It is attractive to butterflies and bees.

❹ Knautia macedonica syn. *Scabiosa rumelica*
Knautia has basal rosettes of leaves and tall, wiry stems topped with dark red flowers. It flowers over a long period in summer.

❸ Malva sylvestris
Common mallow (*Malva sylvestris*) is also a self-seeder and will usually do well in a "wild" planting. It has lobed leaves and pale pinkish-mauve blooms with striped petals.

❻ Lychnis coronaria
Lychnis coronaria makes a basal rosette of gray felted leaves and produces tall branched stems bearing vivid pink flowers. It is not long-lived but seeds itself around.

❺ Centaurea macrocephala
This yellow *Centaurea* has coarse leaves and large flowers like thistles that are good for drying.

EXTRA PLANTS TO CONSIDER: Cranesbill geraniums, *Aquilegia, Camassia, Oenothera, Solidago, Filipendula, Thalictrum*

A grouping of summer perennials on moist fertile soil has been put together here to give color and foliage interest all summer. The plants would look good near a water feature, or with a background of shrubs that enjoy the same conditions.

PERENNIALS FOR A MOIST SITE

They all thrive in partial shade, but the Tradescantia *may flower better with a bit more sun. Remember that moisture-loving plants are happiest when water is constantly present in the soil. If it dries out in the hottest days of summer, then water and mulch, or arrange something to cast shade—either plants alone or a plant-covered structure such as a trellis or pergola.*

A PONDSIDE PLANTING OF contrasting foliage, with the yellow candelabra of *Primula florindae* in the foreground. Its large leaves contrast well with the upright ones of moisture-loving irises and the horizontal line of still water.

SUITABLE SITE: reliably moist, fertile soil in some sun, or partial shade

❶ Lobelia 'Compliment Hybrids'
The bright red, upright flowers of this
Lobelia give good contrast. It has basal
rosettes of dark leaves from which the
flowers rise
in mid to late
summer.

**❷ Carex
elata 'Aurea'**
Further foliage
contrast is
provided by
the sedge
Carex elata. This
form has narrow,
arching leaves in an
attractive yellow-
green. It is
deciduous, but
forms good-sized
clumps when
suited.

**❸ Monarda
'Croftway Pink'**
Monarda has
aromatic leaves and
stiff stems topped
with interesting
whorls of flowers in
midsummer to fall.
It is attractive to bees.

ALTERNATIVE VARIETIES

Lobelia 'Compliment Hybrids'
Lobelia cardinalis 'Queen Victoria'
Monarda 'Croftway Pink'
Monarda 'Beauty of Cobham'
Veratrum viride
Veratrum album or Veratrum
nigrum
Primula florindae
Primula sikkimensis
Tradescantia × andersoniana
'Purple Dome'
Tradescantia virginiana
Carex elata 'Aurea'
Carex oshimensis 'Evergold'

❹ Veratrum viride
Veratrum is essentially a foliage plant, with
unusual pleated leaves and imposing stature.
Prevent slugs or cold winds from spoiling
the leaves.

**❺ Tradescantia × andersoniana
'Purple Dome'**
This Tradescantia has rich purple flowers,
but there are plenty of other colors to
choose from. The leaves can look a bit
untidy. Cut back hard after flowering to
prevent seed formation and encourage
further flowering.

❻ Primula florindae
This giant cowslip flowers in summer above
crinkled leaves up to 18in (45cm) long. Floury stems
carry many sulphur-yellow, fragrant flowers. It looks
at home in marshes and near streams.

EXTRA PLANTS TO CONSIDER: Trollius, Polygonum bistorta 'Superbum', Lysimachia punctata,
Caltha palustris, Geum rivale, Acorus calamus 'Variegatus'

COLORFUL SHRUBS FOR CLAY SOIL

So many plants require well-drained soil that it can be disheartening for people whose gardens have heavy clay soil. The good news is that clay soil is usually fertile and there are shrubs that will grow in it, as long as it does not dry out and become cracked in hot weather. Add bulky organic matter whenever the soil is workable to "open" it and make it more hospitable for root growth. Expect growth to be slower than on more loamy soils.

A mulch of coarse grit discourages slugs and snails and will help to open the soil in time but beware of scorching in hot weather.

HERE *WEIGELA FLORIDA* 'ALBOVARIEGATA' has been underplanted with a blue-green *Hosta* and a delightfully colored *Coleus*. Leaf size and texture also play a part in this grouping. Tender *Coleus* needs to be bedded out after the last frosts, but this does allow the best color contrasts to be chosen.

SUITABLE SITE: sun or partial shade, mulch to improve soil and prevent drying out

❶ Weigela florida 'Albovariegata'

A good contrast to the *Berberis*, this white-variegated *Weigela* has deep pink flowers in summer which also tone with the *Berberis* leaves. It bears its flowers on second-year wood so prune out one third of old shoots each year after flowering.

❷ Berberis thunbergii

Red-leaved barberry has dark purple foliage and stems, with pink-tinged flowers. Red berries appear late, and the leaves color red before falling.

❸ Spiraea japonica 'Goldflame'

The foliage of the *Spiraea* has orange tints when it emerges before turning to golden yellow. Deep pink, fluffy flowers are borne in summer. Cut all the shoots to ground level in spring. Plant two or three together for this grouping.

❹ Chaenomeles × superba 'Knapp Hill Scarlet'

The flowering quince blooms early in spring with scarlet and yellow blossoms on dense twiggy growth. Small yellow fruits may develop later.

EXTRA PLANTS TO CONSIDER: other *Weigela florida* cultivars, *Cotinus coggygria* cultivars, *Philadelphus coronarius* 'Aureus,' *Rosa glauca*

A Sunny Border on Poor Soil

Sometimes it is too difficult to improve the soil of a bed that requires planting, and some soils, such as thin soil over chalk, break down organic matter too rapidly. In these cases choose plants that tolerate poor soil and dry conditions. For larger areas, plant them in groups of each type to give swaths of ground cover. It may be necessary to water them for a while after planting, but once established they will tolerate hot, dry situations.

A RELAXED PLANTING, INCLUDING *Brachyglottis,* on a hot, sunny bank. The line of shrubby plants acts as a barrier between a formal lawn and a lower area of more informal paving. Using plants to cover changes in level is often a more attractive solution than retaining walls or grassy banks.

SUITABLE SITE: poor or light soil in full sun

❶ *Brachyglottis* Dunedin Hybrids 'Sunshine'

Brachyglottis (syn. Senecio) is a tough shrub that grows wider than it is tall, giving good ground cover. It can be cut back to produce denser growth.

❷ *Salvia officinalis* 'Icterina'

'Icterina' is the yellow variegated form of the herb sage. It may be used for cooking, and here it also adds to the yellow color theme.

❸ *Santolina rosmarinifolia* 'Primrose Gem'

The *Santolina* has pretty leaves that contrast well with the larger leaves of the other plants. The little, button flowers are an attractive soft yellow. Cut it back hard in the spring if it begins to grow too lax, although on poorer soil this is less likely to happen. The flowers may fail to appear after hard pruning, but will reappear the following year.

❹ *Ballota* 'All Hallows Green'

The *Ballota* has soft green leaves borne on upright stems. It may be shorn over in spring to keep the growth neat.

❷ *Rosmarinus officinalis* 'Albus'

The rosemary is a culinary herb too, but is useful here for its contrasting form and leaf shape. In hot, dry situations it is wonderfully aromatic.

❷ *Euphorbia myrsinites*

Euphorbia myrsinites is a tolerant plant ideal for the front of hot, dry borders. It has lax stems of glaucous leaves that have a good architectural quality. The limey green flowers are produced on last year's shoots.

EXTRA PLANTS TO CONSIDER: *Lavandula, Rosmarinus, Nepeta, Coreopsis, Salvia*

A Shelter Belt for Mild Coastal Regions

Establishing a wind-break in a seaside garden is a priority if you intend to grow a range of plants. These shrubs are attractive and thrive in mild coastal areas, tolerating salt-laden winds. If your garden needs a long line of defense, plant more than one of each type. The sea buckthorn, Hippophaë rhamnoïdes, *is more likely to produce berries when planted in groups.*

THE FRAGRANT PEA-LIKE FLOWERS of *Spartium junceum* looks stunning against a bright blue sky. Thriving on chalk and tolerating salty winds, it makes a good choice for sunny seaside gardens. Older specimens sometimes grow to look leggy, but may be improved by cutting back hard in the spring.

SUITABLE SITE: any warm open location, not very alkaline soil

ALTERNATIVE VARIETIES

Hippophaë rhamnoïdes
   Escallonia rubia var. *macrantha*
Spartium junceum
   Genista aetnensis
Tamarix tetrandra
   Tamarix ramosissima
Olearia 'Talbot de Malahide'
   Olearia × *haastii*
Griselinia littoralis 'Variegata'
   Griselinia littoralis

❶ *Tamarix tetrandra*
Pink plumes of flowers and feathery foliage give tamarisk an airy look that belies its toughness. It can be kept in good shape by pruning after flowering.

❷ *Hippophaë rhamnoïdes*
Propagating by suckers and with a spreading habit, the sea buckthorn is an excellent wind-break shrub. The leaves are grayish, and orange fruit are produced if planted in groups.

❸ *Spartium junceum*
Spartium, or Spanish broom, is upright and bears a profusion of fragrant yellow flowers in summer. The foliage is sparse, but green branchlets filter the wind and contrast well with the other shrubs.

❹ *Olearia* 'Talbot de Malahide'
Olearia is dense enough to foil any winds. It has abundant, fragrant, daisy-like flowers in late summer above gray-green, wavy-edged leaves.

❺ *Griselinia littoralis* 'Variegata'
Griselinia has pretty waxy leaves that shrug off salty deposits. This variegated one is quite tender inland, but is fine in mild coastal areas as long as the soil is not highly alkaline.

EXTRA PLANTS TO CONSIDER: *Genista aetnensis, Hebe salicifolia, Nerium oleander, Bupleurum fruticosum, Leptospermum laevigatum*

Two types of *Cistus* frame a sundial in a sunny corner. *Cistus* have relaxed, billowing shapes that set off architectural features, as in this picture, and the stiff *Phormium* leaves. Pinch back the tips of new *Cistus* plants to make them grow nicely bushy.

A Windy Garden with Outlook

There are some windy gardens that are too small to accommodate a shelter belt. Or you may not want to wait that long before planting more decorative plants. Often the very situation that makes the site windy also gives wonderful views that would be spoiled with a line of trees or shrubs. The answer is to copy nature's tactics on exposed sites, by growing tough, low-growing plants. If some shelter in the garden is needed, then taller wind resistant plants can be planted to frame the view and shield more delicate species.

SUITABLE SITE: any well-drained soil in sun

❶ *Bupleurum fruticosum*

Bupleurum is evergreen and tough, with yellow-green, starry flowers in domed flower heads that are produced for a long period in the summer. The leaves are blue-green.

❷ *Brachyglottis* Dunedin Hybrids 'Sunshine'

This plant used to be called *Senecio*, and in spite of the name change it is still the familiar, spreading shrub with gray leaves prettily edged with a white line. Some people grow it as a foliage shrub and cut off the flowers. Others enjoy the bright yellow daisies that are produced in summer.

❸ *Erigeron* 'Charity'

'Charity' is a form of *Erigeron* that grows in clumps of mid-green leaves. The pink, semi-double flowers produced all summer are useful for cutting.

❹ *Osteospermum jucundum*

The *Osteospermum* is evergreen with daisy-like flowers that only open in sunshine. The petals are a vivid pinky mauve with a more purple reverse. It is drought tolerant once established, and can be used on wall and banks.

❺ *Phormium* 'Bronze Baby'

For a bit of contrast in form and color, the upright-growing *Phormium* has been added here. It is evergreen with strap-shaped leaves in shades of red and purple.

❻ *Cistus* 'Grayswood Pink'

The common name for *Cistus* is rock rose. It, too, is evergreen, but the leaves are gray-green, and the flowers a silver pink. It is low growing and very hardy.

EXTRA PLANTS TO CONSIDER: hebes, *Santolina*, lavenders, *Helichrysum*

Sometimes the shape of a house, along with an unfavorable aspect and the position of nearby structures, combine to make a really windy, inhospitable environment. Usually these conditions contain a path, so putting up a physical barrier against cold winds is not feasible.

BRIGHTEN A DAMP, WINDY CORNER

To make such an area look more attractive, a tough collection of plants is required. Often it is possible to create a screen using plants. This improves the visual aspect and may reduce the wind enough to grow more delicate things at a later date.

ELEAGNUS PUNGENS 'MACULATA' IS a tough, evergreen shrub that brightens this winter landscape with its yellow variegated leaves. It is larger than 'Frederici' but gives the same effect. Tough evergreens, chosen carefully for leaf form and color, can provide plenty of interest in difficult situations.

SUITABLE SITE: enrich the soil and provide temporary wind protection to get plants started

ALTERNATIVE VARIETIES

Elaeagnus pungens 'Frederici'
   Elaeagnus × ebbingei 'Limelight'
   or 'Gilt Edge'
Hypericum 'Hidcote'
   Hypericum × inodorum 'Elstead'
Viburnum tinus
   Viburnum tinus 'Gwenllian'
Lonicera nitida 'Baggesen's Gold'
   Lonicera nitida
Iris foetidissima
   Iris foetidissima var. *citrina*
Campanula carpatica
   Campanula portenschlagiana

❶ *Elaeagnus pungens* 'Frederici'
Elaeagnus is quick growing for an evergreen, once it gets going, and is tough in the face of cold winds. 'Frederici' is compact and less vigorous, but its variegated leaves are useful to bring a bit of light into shady situations.

❸ *Viburnum tinus*
Viburnum tinus is a very hardy evergreen shrub. It can be hard pruned to suit the situation it is required to fill.

❷ *Hypericum* 'Hidcote'
Yellow flowers over a long period are produced by the *Hypericum*. It keeps its leaves in all but the severest weather.

❹ *Iris foetidissima*
Iris foetidissima has tough sword-shaped leaves giving an upright accent. It has pods that split to reveal red berries later in the year.

❺ *Campanula carpatica*
To furnish the front edge are some hummocks of *Campanula*. It has blue, bell-shaped flowers in summer.

❻ *Lonicera nitida* 'Baggesen's Gold'
The tiny, yellowish leaves of the *Lonicera nitida* are a good contrast, and the airy shrub itself is a lot tougher than it looks.

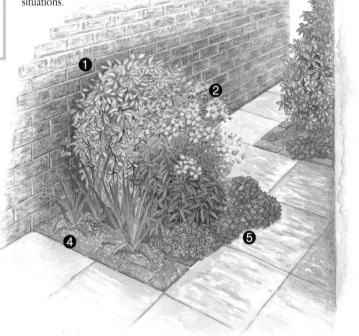

EXTRA PLANTS TO CONSIDER: *Crataegus, Potentilla, Aucuba, Elaeagnus × ebbingei, Helleborus, Convallaria, Tiarella, Galax, Asarum,* hederas

Vinca minor 'Argenteovariegata'
(Periwinkle, Trailing Myrtle)
Trailing stems root where they touch soil, forming good ground cover. Periwinkle flowers produced over a long period. Cut back hard in early spring to restrict growth.

6in x 3ft (15 x 90cm) Shrub
Z4–9 Fertile, moisture retentive, well drained

Weigela florida 'Albovariegata'
Pretty variegated foliage and clusters of trumpet-shaped flowers. It flowers mainly on second-year wood, so prune out one third of shoots to ground level after flowering.

7 x 7ft (2.1 x 2.1m) Shrub
Z4–9 Fertile, well drained

Wisteria floribunda 'Rosea'
Vigorous, woody-stemmed, twining climber, producing long racemes of pink flowers. Grow up a large structure or a tree. Prune and tie in to form a framework of stems. Then, in late summer prune back to 6in of main branches, and again in midwinter to 2 or 3 buds.

28ft, or more (9+m) Climber
Z5–9 Fertile, moisture retentive, well drained

A Note on Latin Names

Many people find using Latin plant names difficult, but they are universally recognized and ensure that wherever you go, whatever language you speak, the full Latin name represents one plant, and one plant only.

ASKING FOR A California lilac in a nursery is simply not accurate enough. Some are large enough to qualify as trees, while others are small enough to plant in a rock garden. Ask for *Ceanothus thyrsiflorus* var. *repens* and you should get exactly what you expect. Don't be embarrassed about pronunciation either. The trick is to say it with conviction, and besides, how many Romans are there around to contradict you? If you really find the names difficult, copy them onto a list and hand it to the assistant at the nursery or garden center. Latin names are the only universal way of identifying plants accurately, so look at them as useful rather than awkward.

Common names are part of our heritage and are often beautifully descriptive. It would be such a shame if names like Lady's Mantle or Bachelor's Buttons were to fall out of usage, but they are often specific to certain regions, and vary from place to place. We should use them when talking informally about our gardens, and reserve the Latin names for technical naming to avoid confusion.

Healthy Plants

If you are choosing containerized plants from a self-serve outlet, look carefully at each one. Each plant should look healthy and full of vigor and be free of pests and diseases.

THE SURFACE OF the compost should be moist and without weeds, moss, and liverwort. There should be no big roots emerging from the holes in the base of the pot, yet there should be enough root growth to anchor the plant firmly in the pot. If you have any doubt, gently knock the plant out of the container to inspect the root system. It should look healthy and be visible at the sides of the pot, but the roots should not be crowded and wound around as though trying to find a way out. This indicates that the plant has been in the pot too long and may be difficult to establish in the soil.

If you have ordered plants to be delivered to your home, unpack them immediately and inspect each one. Inform the supplier as soon as possible if you are not happy with what you find.

ABOVE, HEALTHY *CEANOTHUS* shows a good root system. Before planting, gently tease out some of the roots to encourage them to grow out into the soil.

LEFT, A RED hot poker has become pot-bound, and teasing out the roots would cause too much damage. Avoid buying plants in this condition if possible.

FIRST, IT IS IMPORTANT to rid the soil of all perennial weeds. They are extremely difficult to remove once the plants are established, so be thorough. Use chemicals if you must, but take care to do as little environmental damage as possible.

Most soils will benefit from the addition of organic matter, as explained earlier. This is best done before planting, by adding it as the soil is being prepared. Dig it in as deeply as you like, but avoid disturbing infertile subsoil and bringing that to the surface. The type of organic matter you use is a matter of choice and depends on what is available locally. Try to use recycled materials, such as spent mushroom compost or other by-products of local industry. Make sure they are suitable first, though. For example, mushroom compost often contains chalk, which may alter the pH of your soil significantly. Buying pre-bagged soil conditioners is an alternative, though an expensive one. The best type of soil conditioner of all is the sort you make yourself on the compost heap. The environmental impact of composting may be greater than you think, and it is not difficult once you get the hang of it. It makes little sense to cart your garden and kitchen waste away and then bring in soil conditioners from elsewhere.

A TIMBER-BUILT, DOUBLE compost bin. Timber provides insulation, aiding the composting process. One bin is in use, the other is covered with plastic to keep out rain. The bins are placed out of sight, yet are accessible, with room to use a wheelbarrow for filling and emptying.

COMPOSTING

Learning to make compost is a little like learning to bake a sponge cake. You follow the recipe, and after a few attempts adapt the method to suit your situation. Before long, it becomes second nature. The composting process requires waste plant material, air, and moisture. Success depends on the ingredients being there in the right proportions. In ideal conditions, the temperature will rise enough to kill off weed seeds and complete the process quickly, but perfectly satisfactory compost can be made without the natural heating stage. It just takes longer. For best results, add the materials in layers, and tread them down well. Add water if the heap seems dry and dry materials if it seems too wet. Chop or shred large and woody waste, and add grass and leaves in thin layers or mixed with other things. If the heap does not seem to be rotting down, take it out, mix it up, add more water if it is too dry, or add an activator if all else fails. Put it all back and try again. It is hard work but ultimately far more productive than aerobics! After a bit of experimenting, you will find the best method for you and your garden.

HOW TO PLANT

Once the soil is prepared and the plants are bought and delivered, planting can begin as soon as the weather is favorable. Don't try to plant when the weather is too hot, wet, or frosty.

WATER CONTAINERIZED PLANTS thoroughly by immersing the pots in water until air bubbles cease to rise. Bare-rooted plants should have their roots steeped in water for an hour or two before planting.

Place the pots and their plants in position on the soil according to your plans, and stand back to imagine how big they are going to grow. Make adjustments if you are not satisfied, and then begin to plant.

FOR EACH PLANT, dig a hole big enough to accommodate the whole root system without bending or cramping any roots. If necessary, make a mound of soil in the center of the hole to sit the plant on, allowing the roots to spread out and down into the rest of the hole. There are a few

exceptions to this rule. Some plants benefit from being planted more deeply. This information is given in the cultivation notes in the Plant Directory. Clematis is one example. They benefit from deeper planting because it lessens the likelihood of clematis wilt and promotes the production of more

shoots. Other plants, such as grafted roses, will grow suckers if they are planted too deeply. Try to locate the point of union in grafted plants, and make sure it ends up above soil level. If the plant requires a stake, hammer it in now so that damage to the roots may be avoided.

SUPPORTING PLANTS

Most trees and some shrubs need staking to prevent the wind rocking the root system, causing instability and preventing the roots from working efficiently.

BUY SPECIAL STAKES and ties for this size of plant, as sticks and string are rarely sufficient. Put the stake in the planting hole at the time of planting so that the roots are not damaged. Apply the tie tightly enough to hold the plant to the stake, but not tight enough to cause

rubbing. Advice about the length of the stake and positioning of ties varies, but one current theory is that low stakes that hold the base of the stem and root steady while allowing the stems to move with the wind are best.

Remember to check ties regularly and loosen them as the stem girth increases.

Taller perennials may also require support, especially in windy locations, but for perennials you should wait until the shoots are above ground so that you can see the spread of the plant. Don't leave it too long; stems will never fully recover from wind damage. Begin by putting in supports early and adjust them upward as the plants grow. The supports can then be made the right height to support the plants yet remain hidden by foliage. Supports are available in nurseries, but you can fashion your own from cane or twiggy sticks and string.

ADJUST THE PLANT so that the soil surface is level with the compost in the pot. It may help to lay a stick across as a guide.

BEGIN TO BACK fill with soil, ensuring that there are no air pockets.

WHEN YOU HAVE filled the hole completely, firm the soil thoroughly with your feet.

USE A TREE tie with a buffer to separate the stem from the stake and prevent chaffing. Tighten until firm.

WATER WELL TO ensure soil fills all the spaces around the roots. A shallow dent around the stem will hold water until it soaks in.

MULCH TO A depth of at least 2in (5cm) for a radius of about 2ft (0.6m) to supress weeds and conserve moisture.

A YOUNG STEM of this *Parthenocissus* is being tied to a horizontal wire to encourage it to fill a bare patch on the wall. Left to its own devices it would normally grow vertically to the top of the wall.

heavy, especially if covered with snow, so it is important to provide strong support. The two best methods are either decorative trellising or galvanized wires held up by eyelets screwed to the wall. In either case, leave a gap of approximately 1in(2.5cm) to allow tendrils and twining stems to grow between the wall and the support. When training plants to a vertical support, do not encourage whole stems behind wires or struts, as this may eventually pull the support structure away from the wall. Instead, tie stems to the front of the supports using soft twine or anything that will not rub or damage the stem.

Some climbing plants cling to vertical surfaces by means of aerial roots, or adhesive pads on the shoots. Other climbers need support in order to climb the surfaces you want them to cover. Climbers may become very

FEEDING

THE

SOIL

Most soils require feeding at some time. Nutrients are taken up by plants, and they can be washed out of the soil by water. If plants fail to flourish, have weak growth, sparse yellow leaves, and poor fruit and flowers, then it is quite likely that the soil needs feeding.

IN THIS GARDEN weeds are kept at bay with a mulch of chipped woody material. It will also keep moisture in the soil so that less watering is necessary. A woody mulch of this sort breaks down more slowly than compost, but all organic mulches will eventually enrich the soil.

PLANTS NEED MINERALS from the soil to grow well. The three main minerals are nitrogen (N), phosphorus (P), and potassium (K), and these are required in relatively large amounts.

There are a few different ways to make up any deficiencies. Adding bulky organic matter, like garden compost or manure, is a good method, because it conditions as well as feeds, enabling the soil to hold more moisture. This means that the roots are able to absorb nutrients more efficiently. Other organic fertilizers such as fish, blood, and bone have the advantage of being concentrated and, therefore, easier to apply.

If you are not an organic gardener, concentrated formulations of inorganic nutrients are available. These have accurate proportions of nutrients, and they should be applied carefully to avoid overdosing. They must not be allowed to touch the leaves or they will cause scorching.

Foliar feeds are good for giving plants a boost in the growing season. They consist of soluble nutrients and may be organic, like seaweed extract, or inorganic. Slow-release fertilizers are an efficient way of feeding the soil, though an expensive one. They are granules of fertilizer enclosed in a membrane that becomes more permeable in warm, wet weather. This allows the nutrients to be released into the soil when conditions are favorable for plant growth.

MULCHING

When the plants are planted, watered, and fed, it is usually advisable to apply a mulch. This will deter weed growth, conserve moisture, prevent rapid soil temperature changes, and act as a decorative surface to the soil. Many materials will do; choose one to suit your pocket and the look you require. Shredded bark is attractive and looks good in woodland type settings. Coarse grit or gravel would suit a rock garden or alpine garden. Cheaper but less attractive alternatives in the kitchen garden include straw, newspaper, or old carpet.

In spite of all the care you take in choosing plants, preparing and feeding the soil, planting carefully, and mulching, your plants will get sick from time to time. The best form of prevention is to grow strong, healthy plants that are more likely to shrug off attacks by pests and diseases. The next best method is to be vigilant and catch any problems in the early stages.

PLANT PROBLEMS

THE FIRST STEP is to accurately identify the problem by thorough examination. If it is not obvious, consult a book, ask a more experienced gardener, or take a sample to a nursery for advice.

Infestations of pests or diseases may mean your garden has less than perfect growing conditions; check the requirements of the infected plant and adjust the conditions. If that fails to work, decide on a course of action. Try to use organic methods if you can. They are better for you and the environment. Encourage natural predators such as birds, ladybugs, and garden spiders.

Buy resistant plants if you know you have a problem. Some roses, for example, are more resistant to disease than others. Many gardeners swear by companion planting. French marigolds are often planted next to crops, as they attract aphid eating hover flies.

Clear garden debris where spores and the eggs of pests may lurk. Slugs and snails love the moist environment under garden rubbish.

A NASTY CASE of peach-leaf curl, in this case affecting a wall-trained peach. Keep an eye out for early signs of pests and diseases. Try to identify the problem using reference books or by taking samples to an expert.

Leaves from roses that have been attacked by rust, for instance, are best gathered up and burned.

Specific controls for pests, known as biological controls, are available from specialist suppliers. They may be expensive, but they only affect the target pest and do not harm beneficial insects.

As a last resort you may have to use chemical controls. Use them only if absolutely necessary as they tend to upset the natural balance in a garden, leading to further problems with other pests and diseases. Always choose chemical treatments carefully. Read the labels thoroughly and follow instructions to the letter. Spray in calm weather to avoid drift, and, to prevent leaf scorch, do not use in hot sunshine. Treat all chemicals with respect and protect the environment.

APHIDS, OR GREENFLIES, on a rosebud. If left untreated, they may cause unsightly damage. They also excrete honeydew, which then attract other pests.

MAINTENANCE

Maintaining a newly-planted bed is relatively easy if it was well prepared and then mulched after planting. New plants should not be allowed to dry out, so check the soil periodically. Scrape back the mulch and test how dry the soil is with a finger. It should feel moist to the touch. If not, water thoroughly. Check trees for two or three years after planting, and shrubs for at least a year, especially in dry weather.

WHEN WATERING NEW plants, make sure you give sufficient water to reach the roots. Sprinkling the soil surface may encourage surface rooting, causing problems later in dry weather. Fertilize annually in spring, either with a balanced inorganic product or with well-rotted compost or manure. After

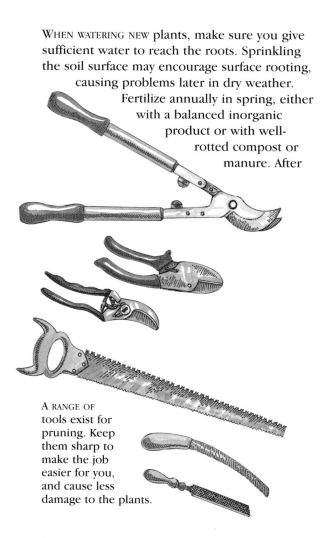

A RANGE OF tools exist for pruning. Keep them sharp to make the job easier for you, and cause less damage to the plants.

fertilizing, and watering if necessary, top up the mulch to a depth of at least three inches. Never apply a mulch to dry or frozen soil, or it will prevent water and warmth from penetrating.

Weeds compete with new plants for water and nutrients, so it is important to remove them as soon as they appear.

Dead-heading, or removing faded flowers, helps many plants as it diverts energy into new growth rather than the production of seeds.

Pruning seems to be a very complicated subject, but if tackled systematically it soon begins to make sense.

THERE ARE FOUR MAIN REASONS FOR PRUNING:

1. To correct any imbalance or remove misshapen shoots. The shrub is then allowed to grow according to its natural habit.

2. To improve flowering, fruiting, and leaf or shoot production.

3. To renovate a neglected specimen.

4. To train a plant, for example, to a support. Trimming hedges is in this category.

It is worth remembering that pruning stimulates increased growth from the buds below the cuts. The harder you prune, the stronger the growth. When trying to put right an unbalanced shrub, prune lightly where you want less growth, and prune hard where you want to promote new shoots. If you are trying to keep a vigorous shrub under control, you may be defeating the object by hard pruning. It may be better to remove it and replace it with something more manageable.

Many shrubs require minimal pruning. This means they may be left alone, except for the removal of dead or diseased shoots that may threaten the health of the shrub.

Deciduous shrubs usually fall into four main pruning categories according to their flowering period and their growth habit, so getting to know your shrubs is important.

1. If they do not regularly produce new shoots from the base, some will require only minimal pruning.

A ROSE BUSH that is overdue for pruning first has all the dead and diseased twigs cut out completely. This makes it much easier to see what else needs to be removed. It also allows air to circulate, making diseases less likely.

THE NEXT STAGE is to remove any stems that cross the center of the plant to prevent them rubbing against each other and causing damage. Finally, any old shoots that flowered last year are removed, encouraging the production of strong new flowering shoots.

2. If they flower in summer or later, shoots produced the same year will require pruning in spring. The aim is to produce vigorous new shoots that will flower later in the season. Neglected shrubs of this sort look congested and do not flower well.

3. Shrubs that flower in spring on last year's growth should be pruned in summer, right after flowering. This gives the plant time to produce new shoots before winter, so that these can produce flowers next spring.

4. If shrubs form lots of new shoots from the base each year, it means they have a natural suckering habit. Once established, they should have one-third of their shoots removed to ground level each spring. The remaining shoots should be cut down to buds that will grow in the right direction to give a good, balanced outline.

While you are carrying out routine maintenance, keep an eye out for suckers on grafted shrubs and reverted shoots on variegated ones. Suckers that arise from below a graft will look different from the rest of the plant. They belong to the rooting stock and will be more vigorous. Left alone they will grow rapidly, to the detriment of the shrub. Scrape away the soil to find the base of the sucker, and pull it away.

Plain green shoots on variegated shrubs have more chlorophyl than the other leaves and will, therefore, be more vigorous. Cut them out as soon as you spot them.

Carried out regularly, this sort of basic maintenance prevents gardening from becoming a chore, leaving you free to sit and survey your achievements or attend to the more creative aspects of gardening.

If in any doubt, there are many good books about pruning that have clear diagrams. The worst thing you can do is give all your shrubs a bit of a haircut and hope for the best. They would probably be better with no pruning at all.

After any pruning, feed your shrubs, and water well in dry weather.

AS WITH MANY variegated plants, this *Lonicera nitida* 'Baggessen's Gold' occasionally produces all-green shoots, which should be cut out as soon as possible.

DESIGNING WITH PLANTS

The truly addictive thing about designing with plants is that it is never completed. You may have planted a border successfully, and yet there is always just that little something extra that would improve it. Perhaps a plant passes its best, or another grows larger than expected. There's a bit of a gap in spring...

IN THIS GARDEN, a formal design has been chosen to contrast with the informality of the natural landscape beyond. Clipped box hedges containing frothy *Dicentra* and domes of a different variety of box create an clean, structured look that does not detract from the informality of the wider, rural view.

DEVELOPING CONFIDENCE WITH plants comes with experience, and experience grows with being observant. Watch your plants and learn all about them and how they interact with each other visually. Stand back and look at them through narrowed eyes to discover their outline. Notice when they look their best, in which sort of light, and at which time of year. Take a sprig and try it against other plants to see how they look together.

Try to analyze what it is that makes your plantings look good, and why things don't work. Take photographs through the seasons to see if a succession of interest is maintained. Photos can have tracing paper placed over them, and sketches made on top to see how new plants would improve the look of a design. If you are stuck for inspiration, garden visiting is a wonderful way to decide which plant combinations please you. Before long, these strategies will help you learn about planting styles, which range from the collector's garden, where all sorts of plants are grown together in haphazard juxtaposition, to the highly structured, minimalist garden. It may be difficult to know how to start developing a style of your own.

A starting place may be to consider the house and its locality. Does the architecture suggest a style? Do the local climate and soil type dictate a certain range of plants?

Even within these constraints, it is still possible to create very different atmospheres with plants. Imagine two identical houses and gardens, one filled to bursting with an eclectic mix of perennials spilling out of the borders and onto the path, and the one next door with a perfect rectangle of emerald grass and a row of pots containing topiary box spheres. Both may suit the style of house and the growing conditions, and yet they conjure wildly different atmospheres.

PLANTS FURNISH A GARDEN

Plants fill a three-dimensional space. Planting is more like sculpting than painting, so try to get to know plants' shapes and varying forms through the seasons.

USE PLANTS TO anchor the house to the landscape, enclose spaces, or frame vistas. Think about the responses plant shapes evoke. Spiky, upright, and mounded plants have different effects. Jagged spiky outlines are exciting, stimulating. Narrow, upright forms suggest movement or activity. Mounds are restful and static. Billowy plants are relaxing, and so on. As we move around a garden, our responses are manipulated by the shapes of plants as much as by their colors or scents. Skilled garden designers use this fact to landscape around buildings, disguising, harmonizing, or complementing architectural features as required.

Less experienced people find it difficult to start. Sometimes it helps to categorize plants according to the function they perform in a design. All borders need a special feature, usually an attention grabbing specimen plant. One is enough, as more than one means they will compete for attention. Position it carefully to emphasize or echo something, or to disguise or draw attention away from an ugly feature.

Next, choose plants to form a skeletal framework, the three-dimensional bulk. They should be quiet performers, made up of evergreens and deciduous plants.

Then fill the spaces with ground-cover plants with good leaf textures and contrasts. These should hold the design together, linking the other elements by threading in and out.

Finally, add some highlights—transient flashes of flowers and sudden eruptions of foliage. Thinking of plants in this sort of hierarchy is another way of putting them together in a visually satisfying way.

THIS GROUPING OF plants (above, left) is satisfying visually because of the use of a restricted range of plants. The gray *Artemisia* forms billows of foliage color, anchoring the *Verbena bonariensis*, which erupts from the gray to give a vivid, yet airy splash of color at a much higher level.

THIS BORDER EFFECTIVELY uses repetition to unify the scheme. Clumps of variegated *Hosta* are spaced along the front edge, with contrasting foliage types giving interest in the background.

DESIGNING A COMPLETE GARDEN

Just as an artist is free to express himself in his painting, you are free to plant your garden any way you want, but arranging plants is designing, and being aware of design principles may help to direct your ideas.

UNITY

This involves the drawing together of unrelated parts into a whole. In a garden this may be achieved in many ways, such as with a style or a color theme. Repetition of a certain feature can unify a design, as can the use of different plants with the same shape.

PROPORTION AND SCALE

The sizes of elements in a planting should relate to each other and their surroundings. Big borders look better with big plants. Small plants can be used in big borders, but they look better planted in large swathes and not singly. Huge leaves would look out of place in a small bed of dainty plants.

SYMMETRY AND BALANCE

Symmetry in plantings brings formality to a design, and informal plantings need to be visually balanced to be successful. For example, a big tree in the distance may need to be counterbalanced by a group of shrubs placed in the foreground.

LIGHT AND SHADE

Try to arrange a balance of light and shade in the garden. This does not have to mean actual sun and shadow, but can be achieved with dark colors, reflective surfaces, and the textural qualities of leaves. Try a shiny-leaved plant under a shady wall, or a purple-leaved shrub alongside a stand of yellow flowers. A balance means that there is relief from glaring brightness and unrelenting gloom.

MOOD AND STYLE

Mood and style reflect highly personal choices, explaining why no two gardens are exactly alike, and why we love some gardens and not others. To a certain extent, fashion influences the way gardens look, but interpretations always vary from person to person.

The atmosphere of a garden depends to a large extent on the planting. A border can have an open, sunny look with lots of bright colors, sparkling leaves, and movement, or it may have a shady mysterious look, with subdued colors and brooding shapes. There may be a very effective transition from one to the other, as a path wends out of the sunlight into the shade.

Style is possibly the most difficult concept to understand. It cannot be achieved by following rules or slavishly copying a look from somewhere else. It is more a distillation of all the influences of climate, culture, geology, architecture, personal taste, and memories, resulting in an influence that guides the design process. Whatever the style which you decide to adopt, it must be carried out with conviction to be successful.

ROSA 'FIRST PRIZE' growing over an arch tempts you to walk along the twisting path to see what lies beyond. The scene is carefully set, with contrasts of light and shade, and sight and scents to beguile.

COLOR

Color coordination in a garden is not as easy as when decorating a room. Light conditions vary so much outside, affecting the way our eyes perceive color, and plants we expect to look good together flower at different times.

COLORS IN THE garden are never seen in isolation, they are always set off by others, especially green, so we can't assess them the way we would if they were on a color chart. When moving plants around in the fall, it is difficult to remember the exact shade of the flowers last June. Color theory is a surprisingly complicated subject, making a color-themed border far from easy. Perhaps it is best to wander around the garden carrying flowers and sprigs of leaves, and mix and match until you come up with satisfying combinations. Making notes is probably the best way of remembering your discoveries, as photographs don't always record exact tones. Many less organized gardeners believe in the saying that "all colors go together in nature." It may well be true, but some combinations are less than charming. It is better to separate blue-pinks from yellow-pinks, for instance. Other clashes will become obvious as you experiment.

Single-color themes are very modish, but difficult to get right. A border of two contrasting colors seems to work better if one of the colors is allowed to dominate, with the other putting in a more restrained appearance. In this way, the dominant color is "lifted" by the other, rather than having to fight with it. Whatever the level of success, it is always enjoyable trying to come up with new and memorable combinations.

THERE ARE SO many flower colors available to the gardener that it can by fun to experiment with contrasts and harmonies. Daily and seasonal changes of light, personal taste, and fashion all contribute to making color use in the garden a fascinating subject.

Color can be used to create other effects in the garden. It is a well-known fact that red seems to advance toward you, making distances look shorter. Blues have the opposite effect. Use this to make a border seem longer, by planting reds in the foreground and blues in the distance. Remember that blues and violets fade rapidly at dusk, so avoid using them around an evening seating area.

Being aware of all the rules and the bits of advice offered by television programs and books should not constrain the way you think about plants. Some of the most successful effects happen when rules are broken and advice ignored. Gardening should be a pleasure, a way of expressing your personality. Create a garden to suit yourself, and enjoy it.

Page references in **bold** indicate entries in plant directory at the bottom of each page.

Quarto would like to acknowledge and thank the following for pictures used on the following pages in this book:

Garden Picture Library: 10t & b;

Jerry Pavia: 3, 28t, 32t, 50t, 54tl, 70t, 74t, 78t, 80t, 82t, 90t, 94t, 98t, 104t, 118, 122, 123t & b, 124;

Harry Smith; 1, 5, 7, 8t & b, 9, 11t & b, 12, 16, 18t, 20t & br, 22t, 24t, 26t, 30t, 32bl, 34t, 36t & bl, 38t, 40t & br, 42t, 44t, 46t, 48tr, 52tl, 56t, 58 t, 60t, 62t, 66, 66c, 68, 71bl, 72t, 73t, 76t, 84t, 86t, 88t, 91br, 95bl, 96t, 99bc, 100t, 102t, 106t & bl, 108t, 110t & br, 112t & bl, 125tl;

Peter Stiles: 16bl, 19br, 22br, 23br, 24bl, 28bc, 31bc, 16bl, 19br, 22br, 23br, 24bl, 28bc, 31bc, 32br, 37bl, 45bl, 46br, 48bl, 49bl, 53bl, 58bl, 59 bl, 63bc, 86bl & bc, 103br, 108bc & br, 112bc, 113br.

All other photographs are the copyright of Quarto Publishing plc

Key
t = top
b = bottom
c = centre
r = right
l = left